African Fusion Cookery

Nina Gaskell

Pen Press

First published in Great Britain by Pen Press

All paper used in the printing of this book has been made from wood grown in managed, sustainable forests.

ISBN13: 978-1-78003-007-4

Printed and bound in the UK
Pen Press is an imprint of Indepenpress Publishing Limited
25 Eastern Place
Brighton
BN2 1GJ

A catalogue record of this book is available from the British Library

Cover design by Jacqueline Abromeit

DEDICATION

"The way to a man's heart is through his stomach", and I therefore, dedicate this book to my husband, in my relentless push to prepare different recipes to stimulate him and excite his taste buds. Also, to friends for their encouragement and to my daughter, Ivy, for her endless nagging to get moving! Finally, to my granddaughter, Yoyo, for her wizardry with the scans and generally helping out Granny on the computer.

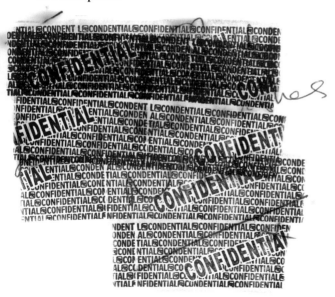

INTRODUCTION

I am grandmother, 3 times over, was born in Nigeria and have lived in the UK since 1963. I came over with the aid of the British Council, who in those days encouraged young people from the Commonwealth to come to the UK to study and develop their skills. I married in 1965 and in the interim the Biafran war broke out in 1967. The war raged for 3 years, and I never went back. My second husband and I have travelled widely, especially since we retired, and the food we have tasted worldwide has inspired me to write a recipe book fusing African ingredients with European and other global influences to create some new and exciting variations on traditional themes. For example, rather than making moussaka in the Greek style, I use plantain instead of aubergine. One of my signature dishes is my black-eyed beans and sweet potato pie, which is very much like a shepherd's pie but with black-eyed beans instead of mince and sweet potato instead of ordinary potato.

I have written this book in the hope that it will appeal to a variety of people especially mothers and those with very lean purse strings. I know sometimes food budgets can be tough on our purses, particularly in challenging economic circumstances, but in my book I've tried to minimise the pain by using less expensive ingredients. Mostly staple store cupboard ingredients and those you can refrigerate for a few days to use in different dishes. They will keep the family happy, healthy and believe you me, they'll be coming back for more!

As you will see, I have used African ingredients in some of my recipes and tweaked it to titillate the English palate. As we live in a cosmopolitan society the ingredients are easily obtainable. I hope this book will appeal to those who have limited time to spend in the kitchen, but who nonetheless enjoy cooking. And, if you're the adventurous type who likes to try something different from time to time, the recipes in my book are certainly for you.

To be a good cook, you've got to have a tidy mind in the kitchen; dirty saucepans, plates and whatever you are using should not be littered all over the kitchen whilst cooking is in progress. Rinse out utensils as you go along. Forget the dishwasher if it's possible.

If you intend to prepare a meal from a recipe book and not by concocting it, always get your ingredients laid out and ready for use. By doing it this way, everything flows and nothing is omitted.

Cooking should be fun and not a chore. If you've some spare time, experiment and be patient, as this is the path of success for all good cooks. Of course, a little bit of imagination also plays an important part. Fearless trial and error is the key.

In my pursuit to improve and enhance the taste of the foods I have prepared, I have discovered 3 main ingredients which I have incorporated in several recipes in this book, i.e. white wine and cream sauce, all-purpose savoury seasoning and palm oil. The palm oil is optional, but if you do use it, make sure it is CSPO or CSPKO certified, i.e. sustainable palm oil, in UK from Asda, Sainsburys, Unilever etc. The combination of white wine and cream sauce with different herbs not only enhances many dishes but it also gives it that extra subtle flavour, whilst the savoury seasoning allows you to use little or no additional salt at all in your cooking.

Sometimes, you may look at a recipe and feel discouraged to give it a go as time is limited to go shopping for the ingredients. My solution is to keep "must have" basic dried ingredients in your cupboard. And these dried ingredients can be anything - mint, parsley, thyme, sage, garlic, bay leaves, basil, paprika, celery salt, coriander, etc.

Also, having frozen vegetables in your freezer enables you to prepare instant meals in no time. During the summer months when vegetables are plentiful, I tend to buy enough to blanch and freeze to use when fresh ones are scarce or more expensive. The vegetables that freeze well are spinach, all kinds of green beans, carrots, cauliflower, and peas. When freezing, use a deep freeze cabinet and not just the frozen food compartment of a fridge. Doing this ensures you have a ready supply of vegetables all year round.

Blanch vegetables for no more than a couple of minutes, drain the hot water and then immerse in cold water until they are cold, not warm. Now drain the water and pack into individual freezer polythene bags.

When ready to use, you do not need to thaw the vegetables, just boil, steam or bake – the choice is yours. Steaming is the healthier option.

In some of the recipes you will notice that I have used supermarkets' own prepared sauces. This is to minimise the time spent in preparing the food.

As we now live in a society where our taste buds have gone through some kind of revolution, I have tried to incorporate ingredients from Africa, i.e. plantain, yam, black-eyed beans, palm oil, okra, etc. into the English cuisine and they are easily obtainable in this country at major supermarkets.

You will notice that there is less of an African influence on the starters in my book than in the rest of the recipes. The reason for this is because African food can be on the heavy side, and generally starters are not eaten, just main courses and desserts. As more Africans become health conscious, perhaps this is no bad thing.

My one great disappointment is that traditional family Sunday lunches have declined over the years - they were a must when I arrived in this country in the early 1960's. For me personally, I would like to see a society where the family makes the effort to have Sunday lunches together, sitting round the table, enjoying the meal and having a good "chinwag". Sadly, many have taken to using their laps as their dining table, which I find abhorrent. We should all try to resist this temptation and eat at the table at least once a week. It instils discipline and manners at the meal table and also helps to develop the family's conversation skills as well as being enjoyable. Above all, better use of cutlery.

Finally, I invite you all to share in the delights of my exciting recipes. And can I say that in life it's difficult to please everybody, but I hope that my ideas will spark some inspiration and ingenuity in everyone's cooking and revive jaded palates.

Bon appétit and happy cooking!

MEASUREMENTS

Note: I always feel that measurements are a guide, i.e. increase or decrease the quantity according to taste. However, where I have used tablespoon or teaspoon, the measurements should not be altered. An example is 3tsp is equal 1tbsp. Below are some additional measurement conversions to help even further:

15g = ½oz; 25g = 1oz; 50g = 2oz; 75g = 3oz; 100g = 3½oz; 125g = 4oz; 200g =7oz; 225g = 8oz; 250g = 9oz; 350g = 12oz; 375g = 13oz; 500g = 1lb.2oz;

Liquid: 150ml = ¼pint; 250ml = ½pint; 500ml = 1pint

Servings: All my recipes are for 4 servings, unless otherwise stated.

OVEN TEMPERATURES

There are always variations in oven temperatures between cookers. Get to know your cooker thoroughly and if you are in any doubt about the temperatures given in some of my recipes, always refer to your own manufacturer's temperature chart.

	Electricity °F	Gas	Fan oven °C
Cool oven	225-250	0-½	107-121
Slow oven	275-300	1-2	135-149
Moderate heat	300-350	2-3	149-177
Moderately hot	400	5	204
Hot oven	425-450	6-7	218-233
Very hot oven	475-500	8-9	246-260

STARTERS

STUFFED MUSHROOMS IN OYSTER SAUCE

As you know, mushrooms in general are not happy on their own. They need that something extra to give them a "kick up the rear" – hence the use of oyster sauce.

This is very simple to make – here we go

Heat oven 200°C/400°F/Gas mark 6

Ingredients:

4 large flat mushrooms
50g butter
1 small onion, chopped finely
2 garlic cloves, chopped
50g coriander or basil chopped and reserve some for garnishing
2tsp oyster sauce
1 small tin sweet corn

Wash the mushrooms and pat dry, then scoop out the flesh, stalk and chop. Melt the butter in a saucepan and fry the onions and garlic until soft. Then add the mushroom flesh and stalks and fry for a further couple of minutes. Now add the sweet corn, coriander or basil and oyster sauce, keep stirring on medium heat for a couple of minutes, take off heat and set aside.

Now rub a little butter in an ovenproof dish. Arrange mushrooms in the dish and spoon the mixture into individual mushrooms. Cover with foil and bake in the oven for 15/20 mins. Remove from oven. To serve, arrange mushrooms on individual plates and if you prefer, thicken the juice with thickening granules or corn flour or, alternatively, just spoon over the juice and serve, garnishing with some chopped coriander or basil.

AVOCADO WITH CHEESE

A straightforward avocado salad with Stilton cheese served with mixed green salad.

Ingredients:

2 ripe avocados
4tbsp French dressing (bought)
1tbsp chopped chives
150g Stilton cheese
½ garlic salt
1tsp coarse black pepper
1 lemon cut into 4 wedges

In a ceramic mixing bowl, mix all ingredients (excluding the lemon). Break the cheese evenly by hand into small pieces and add to French dressing and mix to blend. Meanwhile, cut each avocado in half lengthwise, twist to turn anti-clockwise and remove the stone. Fill the hollowed avocados with the dressing and garnish with lemon wedge.

Surround the avocados with rocket and mixed seasoned salad and serve with some garlic bread.

GARLIC BREAD

Garlic bread freezes very well. Just prepare as below, cool, then wrap in a freezing bag and keep for a couple of days in the freezer.

Ingredients:

1 French loaf
4 garlic cloves, peeled and crushed
1tsp dried mixed herbs
80g butter

Mix garlic, butter and herbs. Cut loaf diagonally 3 or 4cm thick but not right through. Spread butter on one side, then press together. Put in a 425°F/220°C/Gas mark 6 hot oven for a few minutes until the crust is crisp. Serve by cutting into separate pieces.

CUCUMBER WITH GREEK YOGHURT

A plain and simple cucumber recipe for you to enjoy with your favourite salad.

Ingredients:

1 small cucumber cut into small rings
125g Greek yoghurt
1tsp ground coarse black pepper
1tbsp lemon juice
1 large hard-boiled egg (use the yolk only)
½tsp garlic granules (optional)

Arrange sliced cucumber on a plate and sprinkle a pinch of salt all over (this is to rid the cucumber of some of its water). Cover with cling film and rest for about 15 mins and then discard the water. Mix pepper, lemon juice and granules together with half of the yolk. Pour dressing over cucumber and garnish with remainder of egg yolk. Use as an accompaniment to any *al fresco* party.

CARROT BALLS

Eating plenty of carrots makes you "see in the dark", so they say! All the ingredients in this recipe should be staples in your kitchen cupboard for use as and when, apart from carrots, coriander or basil and salad leaves, which of course need to be bought fresh…

Ingredients:

4 medium sized carrots, peeled and grated
1 tsp garlic purée or 1 fresh clove crushed
1 large egg, beaten
1 small onion peeled and chopped finely
50g coriander (use ½tsp of dried one if fresh not available)
2tbsp self-raising flour
1tsp all-purpose savoury seasoning (found in most supermarkets)
Pinch chilli powder (optional)
Green seasoned salad of your choice for dressing
Chinese sweet chilli sauce for drizzling

In a ceramic bowl, mix all ingredients with fork. Rub flour on the palm of your hand. Form mixture into little ping-pong sizes and deep fry until golden. Serve on a bed of green salad and drizzle some Chinese sweet chilli sauce.

NB: do not leave the carrot mixture standing, as the juice will saturate everything.

STUFFED CUCUMBER

This is another delicious way to use healthy cucumbers!

Ingredients:

1 large cucumber, peeled, top and tail then cut into 4 equal sizes
1tsp Tabasco sauce
1tbsp Philadelphia cheese
½ chopped red or yellow sweet pepper
2 shallots peeled and chopped
100g corned beef
½tsp all-purpose savoury seasoning
Black pepper

With a scoop or sharp spoon, gently hollow out the seeds from the cucumber and discard. Now there should be a big enough hole in the middle of the cucumber (resembling a small tube). Mix the remainder of the ingredients thoroughly, fill each cucumber tube with the mixture and slice diagonally thinly. Arrange on a plate one slice overlapping the other and garnish with a seasoned green salad of your choice.

VARIATION – STUFFED TOMATO

Ingredients:

4 firm, medium-sized tomatoes
½ cucumber
2tbsp salad cream
1tbsp white wine vinegar
1tsp coarse black pepper
1tsp mustard
1tsp fresh thyme
Pinch of sugar
100g watercress

Slice tops off tomatoes and scoop out flesh and seeds. Dice half the cucumber and grate the other half. In a ceramic bowl, mix diced cucumber, salad cream, vinegar, pepper, mustard, sugar and thyme. Fill each tomato cup with the mixture. Serve the tomatoes surrounded by the watercress and garnish with the grated cucumber.

Happy summer!

COURGETTE CHEESE SANDWICH

This original courgette sandwich concoction of mine is very popular with my guests and easy to prepare.

Ingredients:

2 medium sized courgettes (about 20 cm long)
300ml fresh cheese sauce – bought (prepare according to instructions)
50g coriander chopped (reserve some for garnishing)
200g (approximately 3) smoked mackerel fillets crumbled.
1tsp coarse black pepper

Heat oven: 200°C/425°F/Gas mark 6

Top and tail the courgettes then cut in half. Trim a bit of the outer layer so that it lies flat. Then cut into 1cm thick slices. Fry dry for 5 mins on both sides to seal. Cool so that it is easy to handle.

Arrange half the courgettes in a buttered ceramic baking dish. Mix fish, coriander and pepper and spread over the courgettes. Then place the remaining courgettes on top, spoon over the cheese sauce. Bake for 20 mins or until brown on top. Serve with the remainder coriander and garnish with black pepper.

SAVOURY SPINACH BALLS

Spinach is one of those leafy green vegetables full of vitamin C and is a good source of iron as well. I remember when I was pregnant (many moons ago) I was advised to eat lots and lots of spinach, to give me enough energy on my day of "pushing". If you happen to buy your spinach from your local market, beware of the grit and give it a good wash in cold water before use. I prefer to buy the prepared packaged ones from the supermarket, as it saves a lot of time.

This recipe could be prepared as a starter, served with Chinese sweet chilli sauce. If you prefer, serve as crudités moulding the spinach mixture into the size of small pebbles held with cocktail sticks and serve with drinks.

Ingredients:

150g spinach
2 large potatoes, peeled, cooked and mashed with cheese and butter
1tsp garlic purée
1tsp all-purpose savoury seasoning
50g Cheddar cheese, grated
1 large egg, beaten
Breadcrumbs for coating
Vegetable oil for deep-frying

Empty spinach into a saucepan and pour boiling water over, cover and allow to cook for about 5 mins. Drain and squeeze excess water with muslin cloth. Add spinach to the potato mixture, all-purpose savouring seasoning and garlic puree then mix thoroughly with fork. Shape into the size of a ping-pong ball, dip in the egg mixture and finally coat the balls with breadcrumbs. Heat oil and deep fry until golden brown – no more than 5 mins or thereabouts.

Serve with Chinese sweet chilli sauce.

NB: *if you are serving as crudités, have chilli sauce as the dip.*

MELON SALAD TOPPED WITH SCALLOPS

This is a simple salad, fresh and crisp to enjoy during the summer months.

Ingredients:

250g sweet Galia or Cantaloupe melon
50g fresh basil, chopped
150g crisp Cos lettuce (break evenly with your hands)
1tbsp clear honey
1tbsp lemon juice
8 fresh scallops
½ red peppers, deseeded and cut into little squares
2tbsp olive oil
1tsp fresh ground black pepper
1tbsp Cajun spice or Chinese five spice

Peel melon, deseed and cube into a bowl. Mix honey, olive oil, lemon juice, basil and black pepper, and then add the melon and sweet pepper; toss and rest.

Meanwhile prepare scallops - toss in Cajun spice and fry in heated olive oil for a minute on both sides, then cover and rest.

You need 4 cooking rings – 90mm x 35mm. Fill each ring with the prepared melon then follow with the lettuce leaves. Press down lightly and top with the fried scallops. Lift the rings, drizzle the juices from the melon over the salad and serve immediately.

BAKED BUTTERNUT SQUASH

This is a recipe given to me by a South African friend of mine, but I have adjusted it accordingly. I just love the texture of the squash when cooked and I hope you will like my version of baked squash.

Ingredients:

850g butternut squash
4 ovenproof scallop dishes – 6" across
6 dry cured smoked bacon rashers – cut into little pieces
1 red pepper, deseeded and chopped
1tsp all-purpose savoury season
50g coriander, chopped including the stalk (reserve some for garnishing)
1 medium onion – chopped
1tbsp olive oil or butter
Cheese of your choice, according to taste

Heat oven
220°C/425°F/Gas mark 7

Peel squash and cut into large cubes. Boil for about 15/20 mins or until tender. Drain, add butter and mash. Add chopped onions, bacon, pepper, coriander, all-purpose savoury seasoning and the olive oil. Mix well with a wooden spoon and then fill each shell with the mixture, top with the cheese. Bake for 15/20 mins or until brown on top. Garnish with the remainder of the coriander and serve immediately.

AVOCADO and ROCKET SALAD

Another avocado recipe for you! Nice and light for the summer months.

Ingredients:

2 small carrots, peeled and grated
2 ripe avocados, stoned
200g king prawns – reserve 8 for garnishing (2 each)
1tbsp salad dressing of your choice
1tsp olive oil
50g rocket
1tsp sesame seeds
1tsp coarse black pepper

Mix all ingredients excluding the sesame seeds. Have 4 cooking rings ready for shaping the salad on each plate. Arrange rocket leaves first, pile on mixture, garnish with prawns, in a criss-cross pattern, and finally scatter some sesame seeds on top.

OR

If you do not fancy this recipe, why not try this:

Ingredients:

1 small cabbage, shredded
1 avocado, stoned and cut into cubes
1 small tin of pineapple (in juice not syrup), drained
2tbsp salad dressing of your choice
Salt and pepper

Mix thoroughly and serve

Serving suggestion - try piling the salad mixture into white crusty rolls making a quick tasty snack?

STUFFED SAVOURY GREEN PEPPER WITH SMOKED MACKEREL

Stuffed peppers are such an easy dish. You are spoilt for choice as to what to include in your stuffing. It can be rice, meat, fish or even mixed vegetables, chopped very finely, mixed and seasoned. In this recipe I am using fish for a change. You can scoop out tomatoes, courgettes or even aubergines and use in the same way.

Set oven: 190°C/375°F/Gas mark 5

Ingredients:

2 medium-sized green peppers
4 small filleted smoked mackerel
1 clove garlic, peeled and pressed
1 small onion, peeled and chopped
2 ripe tomatoes, skinned and chopped
1tbsp white wine and cream sauce
1tbsp olive oil
1tsp all-purpose savoury seasoning
1tsp paprika (optional)

Preheat oven. Cut pepper in half, lengthways and scoop out the seeds. Heat oil and fry all ingredients for about 5 mins and add the wine sauce and savoury seasoning for a further 5 mins on slow heat. Then add bite-sized mackerel pieces to the sauce and simmer for a further 5 mins. Check seasoning and remove from heat.

Spoon mixture into each pepper and arrange in oven-proof dish. Drizzle with some more olive oil and black pepper, cover with foil and bake for 20 mins. Five minutes before the end, increase oven heat, remove the foil and let the edges brown a little. Serve garnished with watercress and the remainder of the juice from the dish.

PLANTAIN and HARICOT BEAN PATTIES

This recipe is just one of many ways to combine plantain and haricot beans. I have created these lovely patties, which I believe could definitely blow your mind! This is a particularly delicious recipe, combining the more starchy plantain with the fluffy texture of the beans. It can be served on its own with chilli sauce or as a light supper with salad.

Ingredients:

1 ripe yellowy plantain
1 small tin of haricot beans (about 100g)
2 Weetabix biscuits, crumbled
2 medium sized eggs, beaten
1 medium onion, peeled and chopped
50g coriander or ½ tsp dried or basil
2 garlic cloves, peeled and pressed with garlic press
1 yellow or red sweet pepper, deseeded and finely chopped
1 chicken stock cube, (crumbled) – vegetarians can substitute a vegetable stock
Flour for coating
Vegetable oil for frying

Peel and chop the plantain, then place in a ceramic mixing bowl and mash. Add all the ingredients (with the exception of the flour and oil) mix well with a wooden spoon. When blended, cover with cling film and rest for 30 mins. When ready to cook, flour your palms, divide the mixture and shape each portion into the size of a golf ball. Heat enough oil and fry in batches over medium heat, turning once, until golden on both sides. Drain on kitchen paper to absorb excess oil. Serve with seasoned green salad of your choice together with Chinese sweet chilli sauce.

Bon appétit!

AUBERGINE AU GRATIN

This is very simple recipe for a mid-week meal with your family. Quick to prepare with little fuss. Vegetarians can of course replace the bacon or ham with a Soya meat substitute, as well using a vegetarian hard cheese instead of Parmesan.

Ingredients:

2 large aubergines cut lengthways 10cm thick
8 medium tomatoes, skinned and chopped
3 garlic cloves, chopped
6 slices smoked bacon, chopped or ham if you prefer
1 medium onion
2 tbsp olive oil
50g basil or coriander, chopped
150g Gruyère cheese, grated
50g Parmesan cheese, grated
1 tbsp white wine and cream sauce

Heat oven: 200°C/400°F/Gas mark 6

Wash aubergines then top and tail. Cut lengthways and fry dry to seal.

Meanwhile, heat the oil in a saucepan. Fry the onion and garlic on medium heat for a couple of minutes then add the tomatoes, bacon, coriander, white wine and cream sauce on medium heat for about 3 mins. Season with salt if required.

Now grease an ovenproof dish with some olive oil and line with some of the prepared aubergine (about 4 or thereabouts). Spread half of the cooked sauce over them, then half the grated Gruyère cheese. Place another layer of aubergine on top, followed by the remainder of the sauce and the Gruyère and Parmesan cheese. Bake for 25/30 mins until brown on top.

Serving suggestion: as a side dish to your baked aubergine, try serving with some fried or grilled plantain.

SOUPS

HOT AND SOUR SOUP

This is a rather fiery soup – nothing better to enjoy during those cold winter months, with some crusty garlic bread. Mmmmm, it's 'luvelly'!

Ingredients:

3 sweet yellow peppers (or red), deseeded and chopped
1 thumb size ginger, grated
1tbsp white wine vinegar (you can use ordinary vinegar or if neither are available, use 1tbsp lime juice)
1 medium onion, chopped
1 level tsp Harrisa paste – you can get it from any supermarket
3 garlic cloves, peeled and chopped
2tbsp vegetable oil
1 chicken (or vegetable) stock, dissolved in one litre of warm water
Coriander leaves for garnishing

Heat oil in a pan and fry the ginger, garlic and onions for about 3 mins. Add the chopped yellow peppers and cook for about 1 minute. Now add the remainder of the ingredients, bring to boil and simmer until the peppers are tender (about 15 mins). Check seasoning, then liquidise. Put through a sieve then heat through again (do not boil). Serve sprinkled with coriander leaves and serve with any crusty bread of your choice.

PEA AND POTATO SOUP

This is my version of pea soup – very warming. Subtly seasoned – serve with croutons for a real soup lover's treat!

Ingredients:

450g frozen peas
1 large potato (or 2 medium), peeled and cubed
50g chopped, fresh mint or 2tsp dried mint
2tbsp vegetable cooking oil
1 small onion, peeled and chopped
2 garlic cloves, skinned and chopped
1 thumb size ginger, finely chopped or 1tsp dried ginger
1 vegetable or chicken stock, dissolved in 700ml of hot water.
2tbsp white wine and cream sauce (this is available from most supermarkets – freeze the rest for use as and when).

Heat the oil in a pan and fry the ginger, onions and garlic for a couple of minutes. Then add the cubed potatoes, stir and add stock. Simmer for about 5 mins, then add the peas, ½ the chopped mint and the cream sauce. Simmer for about 20 mins or until potatoes are tender. Check seasoning. Cool, liquidise, then sieve. Return to saucepan to reheat. Sprinkle the remainder of the fresh mint on each soup bowl to garnish.

NB: *if you have any leftover cream in the fridge, drizzle a little in each bowl or alternatively a dollop of natural yoghurt before serving. Add a handful of croutons if you fancy some crunchiness.*

Enjoy!

MANGE TOUT PEA SOUP

Mange tout is an underused vegetable in English cooking, but is very popular with the Chinese. It's a very versatile vegetable, which can be eaten raw. Sometimes referred to as snow peas, they are full of vitamin C. Brilliant in mixed green salad. Generally, they need to be stir fried for just a couple of minutes to retain their crispness. In this recipe, however, I'm not stir frying, but instead making a delicious winter *Willy warmer* soup.

Ingredients:

240g mange tout (washed, topped and tailed) - reserve a couple for garnishing
2tbsp vegetable cooking oil and 1tsp palm oil
1tsp chilli flakes (optional)
2tbsp Philadelphia (or other soft) cheese
1 small onion, chopped
2 garlic cloves, peeled and chopped
1 stock cube (vegetable, chicken or beef) dissolved in 600ml of warm water
1tsp tomato puree

Fry the onion and garlic in a pan, on a medium heat for a couple of minutes. Add the mange tout, followed by the stock, tomato puree, and cheese and simmer for 15 mins. Check seasoning. Remove from the heat and allow to cool. Liquidise and put through sieve. Return to heat, (do not boil) taste and add seasoning if necessary. Serve garnished with thin strips of the mange tout and finish off with chilli flakes if you prefer.

CUCUMBER SOUP

Poor cucumber - you're so bland, you need a helping hand and a kick up the backside! I'm bringing you to life with my recipe. Having said that, they're full of nutrition and you can eat as much as you like, without having to worry about weight gain. Not only are they good for cholesterol, they settle the stomach if you suffer from acidity.

Ingredients:

1 cucumber, peeled, cut in half, deseeded and cut into small pieces (reserve some of the peeled skin for garnishing - cut into thin 2cm strips)
1 chicken or vegetable stock, dissolved in 500ml of warm water
2tbsp Philadelphia (or other soft) cheese
1 onion, peeled and chopped
1 sweet red pepper, deseeded and chopped
2tbsp vegetable oil
2 garlic cloves, peeled and chopped
50g fresh coriander, chopped (remove stalks) or 1tsp of dried
Salt and pepper

Heat the oil and fry the onion and garlic for a few minutes. Gradually add the stock and bring to the boil. Add cucumber, salt, pepper, red pepper and coriander and simmer until cucumber is tender. Cool then liquidise. Pour soup through a sieve, then return to the pan. Now add the Philadelphia cheese and stir to blend (do not boil). Check seasoning, serve immediately garnished with strips of cucumber skins.

BLACK-EYED BEAN SOUP WITH PALM OIL

Black-eyed beans are one of the most common beans eaten in Nigeria. They have a lovely creamy, fluffy texture when cooked. They can be used in so many different ways i.e. in soups, to garnish salads, cooked together with rice as they do in the Caribbean or simply eaten on their own with a little Creole sauce if you prefer. This is a healthy soup that is full of protein and fibre.

Ingredients:

100g tinned black-eyed beans (haricot beans work equally well) - rinse under cold tap to remove preservatives
50g button mushrooms
3 medium sized tomatoes, skinned, deseed and chopped
2 small carrots, peeled and cubed
2 or 3 celery sticks
1tbsp palm oil
1tbsp vegetable oil
500ml chicken (or vegetable) stock
3 cloves garlic
1 small onion, peeled and chopped
1 green chilli, deseeded and chopped
Salt and black pepper
Parmesan cheese to garnish

Peel and chop the carrots into small pieces. Heat oil and sauté carrots on low/medium heat for 5/6 mins, stirring intermittently. Add the onions, garlic, tomatoes and chilli and sauté for a further 5 mins, then add the stock and the beans. Season well with salt and freshly ground black pepper. Bring to boil and simmer for 15 mins to enable fusion to take place. Liquidise half the mixture, then empty this into the other half. Warm through. Serve immediately with grated Parmesan and some hot, crusty garlic bread.

NB: if you find the consistency too runny, thicken with come corn flour.

SOY SAUCE SOUP

I came about making this soup simply by experimenting with some left over vegetables, and this is the result. This is a thick, creamy soup, perfect for when those cold evenings descend on us once more, and very easy to prepare.

Ingredients:

3 large carrots, peeled and cut into medium sized cubes
1 large parsnip, peeled and diced
2 cloves garlic, chopped
4 medium tomatoes, skinned and chopped
1 medium onion, chopped
2 tbsp olive or sunflower oil
50g coriander, reserve some leaves for garnishing
1tbsp soy sauce
1 chicken stock made up to 750ml
1 tbsp white wine and cream sauce

In a saucepan heat the oil and fry the onions and garlic on a medium heat for a couple of minutes. Add tomatoes, carrots, parsnips, coriander, soy sauce, white wine and cream sauce and chicken stock.

Bring to boil and simmer until vegetables are tender. This should take no more than 15/20 mins.

Take off heat and cool. Liquidise in blender until smooth. Return to saucepan and add salt and pepper if required and keep stirring on low heat until fully reheated. Do not boil. Garnish with the remainder of the coriander and serve.

NB: if after liquidising the soup, you find the consistency too thick, just add a little warm water before serving, stir and serve.

PARSNIP AND CELERY SOUP

One Christmas, I found I had an abundance of vegetables left over and instead of simply throwing them in the bin, I put them to good use by making this appetising soup. If you love parsnips and celery, you will undoubtedly love this soup!

Ingredients:

600g parsnips, peeled and cut into medium chunks
3 celery sticks, diced - reserve some leaves for garnishing
1 large onion, peeled and chopped
3 cloves garlic, peeled and chopped
4 large tomatoes, skinned, deseeded and chopped or you can use a small tin of chopped tomatoes
2 tbsp vegetable oil
1 chicken or vegetable stock cube, dissolved in 750ml of hot water
150ml single cream
Crushed black pepper for garnishing

Heat oil and fry the garlic and onions for a few seconds, then add the tomatoes, chopped parsnips and celery. Stir on a medium heat for about 5 mins. Now add the stock, stir and bring to the boil. Reduce heat and simmer gently until the vegetables are tender. This should take no more than 20/25 mins Check seasoning. Remove from heat and cool. Transfer to a blender and liquidise.

Empty contents back into the saucepan, stirring half the single cream into the soup. Warm through gently (do not boil) and serve in warmed soup bowls. Drizzle remainder of cream in each bowl and garnish with the chopped celery leaves.

NB: if you find the consistency too thick, add a little warm water, check seasoning before serving.

TOMATO, COCONUT MILK and
BAKED BEANS SOUP

I went to my local market, bagged myself some ripe tomatoes, but unfortunately too many for my purpose. Reluctant to waste them, I ended up using the remainder to create this unique, individual soup with its combined English and oriental flavours.

Ingredients:

500g ripe tomatoes, skinned, deseeded and chopped
50g flat leaf parsley or coriander, chopped reserve some for garnish
200g tinned baked beans
1 medium onion, peeled and chopped
2 garlic cloves, peeled and pressed or chopped
1 thumb sized ginger, grated
300ml coconut milk
1 chicken or vegetable stock cube, dissolved in 300ml of warm water
1tsp paprika
2tbsp sunflower or vegetable oil

Heat the oil and add the onions, garlic and ginger and cook for a couple of minutes. Add tomatoes, milk, stock, paprika, parsley or coriander, bring to boil and simmer for about 15 mins. Add baked beans. Check seasoning, adding salt and coarse black pepper if necessary. Remove from heat, cool and liquidise. Return to heat, but do not boil. Serve in warmed soup bowls, topping with coriander.

Delicious!

BUTTERNUT SQUASH AND
FRENCH BRIE SOUP

My husband treated himself to some French Brie and having told him off about its pungent smell, to appease me, he suggested that I make some soup with the remainder. Lo and behold, this was the end product!

Ingredients:

800g butternut squash (roughly a whole medium-sized butternut squash)
50g coriander or flat leaf parsley
4 medium tomatoes, skinned and chopped
2 garlic cloves, chopped
1 medium onion, chopped
1½ chicken or vegetable stock cube, dissolved in 750ml warm water
60g French Brie (remove the rind)
2 tbsp sunflower or vegetable oil
1 thumb-sized ginger, chopped

Cut the squash in half (for easy handling) and peel, deseed and cut into cubes. Heat the oil and fry the onion, garlic and ginger for about 1 min. Then add the tomatoes, squash and coriander or parsley and simmer gently for about 3 mins. Now add the stock and Brie, bring to the boil and simmer gently for about 20/25 mins or until squash is tender. Cool slightly then liquidise until smooth. Return to saucepan and warm through thoroughly before serving.

You can either serve the soup immediately after liquidising and enjoy it with all the cheesy residue (as does happen). Or, if you prefer a smoother consistency or perhaps simply want to avoid the residue sticking in between your falsies (i.e. one's "National Health Gnashers" if you wear them!) put the liquidised soup through a sieve before serving.

Serving suggestion: why not try it with some delicious Melba toast?

Don't buy the supermarket versions, make your own as it is tastier, has no preservatives and is easy-peasy!

Pre-heat the grill. The amount of bread you use is up to you. Toast thick slices of bread with the crust still on in a toaster or if you prefer under the grill on both sides. Trim the crusts off the bread once toasted and straight away, gently place your palm on the toasted bread and with a sharp knife, cut through the slices horizontally, leaving you with one toasted and one untoasted side. Place untoasted side up under the hot grill until they curl up. Be careful as you slice!

Serve immediately.

ASPARAGUS and PALM OIL SOUP

Let's go African with this soup!

250g asparagus, washed and cut into small pieces – reserve some cooked spears for garnishing.
180g potatoes, peeled and cut into cubes
4 medium tomatoes, skinned and chopped
1 medium onion, chopped
2 garlic cloves, chopped
1 green chilli, deseeded and chopped (optional)
1 tbsp palm oil
1 tbsp vegetable or sunflower oil
2 medium or 1 large red pepper, deseeded and chopped
1½ chicken or vegetable stock cubes made up in warm water to 700ml
Salt

Heat the oil, fry the onion and garlic for a couple of minutes then add the tomatoes, potatoes, asparagus, chilli and red pepper and simmer on medium heat for about 5 mins. Now add the stock, bring to boil and simmer for about 20 mins.

Take off heat and allow to cool. Liquidise in a blender. Return to the saucepan and check seasoning. Reheat thoroughly but do not boil. Garnish with the remaining asparagus spears.

ORANGE and TOMATO SOUP

The humble tomato is one of our most popular vegetables and incredibly versatile – although, yes, technically, it is a fruit! You can eat them raw, add them to salads and sandwiches, bake them, use them as a base for sauces or generally in whatever takes your fancy really! You can even make a refreshing summer drink by juicing them and adding some herbs, e.g. mint along with some ice. Packed full of vitamins and anti-oxidants, all in all, you cannot go wrong with tomatoes. But a word of warning - tomatoes are very acidic, so if like me you suffer from the production of too much acidity in your stomach, go easy tiger!

Give this flavoursome recipe a try - I hope you like it!

Ingredients:

900g tomatoes, skinned, deseeded and chopped
Juice of one orange
1 medium onion, peeled and chopped
2 garlic cloves, peeled and crushed
50g basil, reserve some for garnishing
1½ chicken or vegetable stock cubes, dissolved in 750ml warm water
1tsp crushed ginger
2tbsp vegetable or olive oil

Heat the oil, and fry the onion, garlic and ginger for a couple of minutes on a medium heat. Add the stock, tomatoes and basil and simmer for 10/15 mins uncovered. Check seasoning. You may need a little bit of salt to taste. Before liquidising, add the orange juice. Return to heat and warm through thoroughly. Garnish with the remainder of the basil and serve.

POTATO SOUP

This is a very simple and nifty little recipe I devised with busy mums in mind – something quick and easy to prepare for their kiddiewinks! It is a very light supper to have ready when they return home from school and before they start screaming, "Mum! I'm hungry!" It takes no more than 20mins from start to finish. So come on, let's get cracking! And no excuses - forget bags of fatty crisps and biscuits. Of course, you don't *have* to be a busy mum or a ravenous child to enjoy this hearty soup!

Ingredients:

1 large potato, peeled and grated
1 chicken or vegetable stock, dissolved in 500ml of warm water
1 medium onion, peeled and chopped
2 tbsp vegetable oil
Salt and pepper
A handful of cabbage if you have any lurking in your fridge

Heat the oil and fry all ingredients for a couple of minutes. Add the stock, bring to the boil and simmer for 10/15 mins. Season to taste, stir well, cool and liquidise. Return to heat, warm through thoroughly and serve.

There you have it!

SWEET RED PEPPER SOUP with
COCONUT MILK

I use a lot of green and red peppers in my cooking and have been buying them at my local market for many many years. When I go to the market late on Saturday afternoons, my favourite stallholder often fills my bag up with freebies he does not want to take home with him. The moral is – cultivate a friendly rapport with your local greengrocer!

This recipe came about when, on one occasion, he gave me a big bag of red peppers and I was wondering what to do with them. After much thought and a flash of inspiration, this recipe was born! My husband loves this soup and thinks it's "smashing." I hope you do too.

Ingredients:

8 medium sweet red peppers or 6 large ones, deseeded and chopped into little pieces
2tbsp vegetable or olive oil
1 medium onion, peeled and chopped
1 chicken or vegetable stock dissolved in 500ml of warm water
2 garlic cloves, peeled and crushed
125ml coconut milk (reserve some for drizzling over soup)
50g basil chopped
Salt and coarse black pepper

Heat the oil and fry all ingredients, with the exception of milk, stock and basil on medium heat for a couple of minutes. Add the stock, milk and basil, bring to boil and simmer for another 15 mins. Check seasoning. Slightly cool and liquidise. Drizzle the remaining coconut milk over the soup in a circular swirl and serve.

Absolutely mouth-watering!

CELERY and TOMATO SOUP

This soup is full of soul and goodness. So tasty! The addition of soy sauce turned it downside up… A real winter warmer!

Ingredients:

450g ripe medium tomatoes, skinned and chopped
2 small potatoes, peeled and cut into small cubes
1 medium onion, peeled and grated
1tbsp sugar
1 chicken or vegetable stock cube, dissolved in 500ml of warm water
2 garlic cloves
1 thumb-sized ginger, grated
100g celery stalks, chopped
2tbsp vegetable oil
1tbsp soy sauce
A little grated Parmesan or Cheddar cheese, for garnishing
Salt and coarse black pepper

Heat the oil, add the onion, garlic and ginger and cook for 3 mins, stirring. Add tomatoes, potatoes and celery stalks and cook for a further 5 mins. This should be followed by the stock, sugar and soy sauce and simmer for a further 15/20 mins or until the potatoes are cooked. Check seasoning. Remove from heat, cool then liquidise. Put through a sieve. Reheat to warm through and serve garnished with the cheese.

This soup works particularly well with warm, crusty bread.

MAIN COURSES

BLACKEYED BEANS AND SWEEET POTATO PIE - *"AKIDI"*

This is a hip-hop, budget-friendly dish for the whole family to enjoy! It's a very simple recipe, full of flavour. I like to place it in the middle of the dining table for every member of the family to tuck in.! It is my version of the traditional English Shepherd's pie using black eye beans instead of mincemeat.

Ingredients:

225g black-eyed beans: (no need to soak overnight)
1 sweet red pepper, deseeded and chopped
1 medium sized onion, peeled and chopped
2 garlic cloves, peeled and chopped
1 thumb-sized ginger, grated
1 chicken or vegetable stock cube, dissolved in 50ml warm water
½ tin chopped tomatoes
1tsp ground paprika
3 tbsp sunflower or vegetable oil
50g Parmesan or Cheddar cheese, grated
2 medium sized Kumara sweet potatoes,

50g butter
50g coriander or basil, chopped, set aside a handful for garnishing
1tsp curry paste (optional) if you fancy that extra kick!

Heat oven: 190°C/375°F/Gas mark 4

Peel and cube the sweet potatoes, then boil for 15 mins until soft. Add butter and mash with a potato ricer to achieve a smooth finish, then put to one side. Boil the beans rapidly for 5 mins, drain and rinse under cold running tap to rid the beans of the dark cooking water. Add water to cover the beans again, bring to boil and simmer for about 20/25 mins, until soft. Meanwhile fry the onion, garlic and ginger on a medium heat for 3/5 mins. Now add the tomatoes, sweet peppers and paprika and simmer for a further 5/10 mins stirring intermittently. Add the stock together with the coriander and simmer for a further 5 mins. Check seasoning. Empty cooked beans into the sauce, and stir well to blend. Pour the entire contents into a ceramic baking dish, top evenly with the mashed sweet potatoes and sprinkle all over with the grated cheese. Bake in the oven for 20 mins until golden brown.

This is a lovely recipe for both veggies and non-veggies and highly nutritious. Have it with a bowl of your favourite seasoned green salad, or meat eaters might want to try it with some salmon, chicken or steak to increase the protein element.

NB: you can now buy ready-cooked beans from supermarkets to save time, but you must rinse thoroughly under a cold tap, to remove all traces of preservatives before use.

YAM GOULASH

The yam is one of Africa's staple foods, enjoyed widely throughout the continent. Rich in carbohydrate it is quickly filling due to its high starchy content.. Yam is grown the same way as potatoes. They are much bigger however, and have a rough, brownish skin. When cooked, they closely resemble Maris Piper potatoes in texture. But this is where the potato comparison ends as yam has a unique taste all of its own. African yams are totally different in texture from those you find in the West Indies and should also not be confused with sweet potatoes. To titillate your taste buds and perhaps introduce you to this most distinctive vegetable, I have created this goulash, incorporating some spicy European influence in the form of paprika and chorizo. Vegetarians may add a soy or meat substitute sausage of their choice – the spicier the better! You may have to head to an Indian or African grocery shop to purchase the yam.

Ingredients:

600g yam, peeled and cubed
4 large tomatoes, peeled, deseeded and chopped
100g chorizo cut in half
1tsp paprika
2tbsp vegetable oil
1 chicken or vegetable stock cube, dissolved in 700ml warm water
1 medium onion, peeled and chopped
2 garlic cloves, chopped
1 thumb-sized ginger, chopped
260g young spinach
Salt and black pepper

Heat the oil and lightly sauté the onion, garlic and ginger. Add the tomatoes and cook for a further couple of minutes. Add the yam followed by the stock, paprika and chorizo. Bring to the boil rapidly then reduce to simmer for 15 mins. Check yam for softness – once tender, add the spinach and cook for a further 5 mins until the spinach is cooked, stirring intermittently to blend. Check seasoning. Easy does it!!

This is a complete meal in itself, but you can add a piece of cooked chicken, steak or fish, if you prefer.

Keep cooking and be happy!

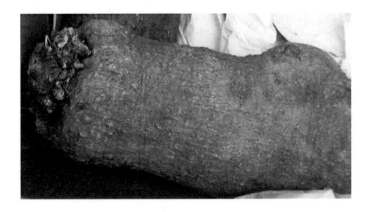

MEAT BALLS

A simple, classic meatballs dish, easy to prepare and very economical. Full of flavour and nourishing. One at which the children will not turn their noses up - yum!

Ingredients:

200g minced beef
200g minced pork
1 medium onion, peeled and chopped
2 garlic cloves, peeled and crushed
2tbsp tomato puree
2tbsp white wine and cream sauce
½tsp dried thyme or rosemary
1 large egg
2tbsp vegetable oil
100g baby spinach (bought already prepared in supermarket)
1 chicken stock dissolved in 250ml warm water
Baking flour

Mix the beef, pork, onions, garlic and herbs together in a large bowl, then add the beaten egg to bind. Empty the meat mixture onto a floured board and with floured palms, roll into small balls. Heat some oil in a large frying pan and when hot, add the meatballs until slightly browned. When evenly brown, add the stock together with tomato puree and white wine and cream sauce. Bring to the boil then simmer for 10 mins. Add the spinach and simmer for a further 5 mins. Check seasoning. Leave to stand for a couple of minutes before serving.

Serve with some buttered mashed potatoes.

SLOW COOKED BRISKET

This is a budget friendly dish. Brisket is the forgotten part of beef that we don't generally bother with! However, this part of beef is so sweet, full of flavour and very cheap. 1kg is enough for a family of 4, save the rest of the cooked brisket for a midweek shepherd's pie special! Possibly brisket is often overlooked because of its toughness, but you can easily overcome this if you let me show you how. I am now appealing especially to cooks to try this cut my way: on a Sunday before leaving home to join your kiddiewinks play their football game, why not wake up early, put the oven on, prepare the beef, i.e. season the same, bang it in the oven, forget about it for about 4 hours, by which time it'll be ready for you and your family to enjoy a succulent Sunday roast and doze off in front of the telly…

Ingredients:

1kg brisket
3tbsp gravy granules
1 small onion peeled and chopped
2 garlic cloves, peeled and chopped
700ml warm water
2 celery sticks, chopped
100g (about 2) carrots, peeled and cubed
Salt and pepper
Corn flour

Heat oven: 150°C/350°F/Gas mark 3

The beef should be at room temperature before seasoning with salt, pepper and corn flour. Dry fry on a medium heat to seal all over, turning intermittently until brown. In a saucepan, dissolve the gravy granules in water, add the remainder of the ingredients, bring to boil and simmer for about 5 mins. Empty the beef contents into a ceramic stew pan, cover with greaseproof paper and put the lid on top. Place at the bottom of the oven and allow to braise without interruption for 3½ hours. For the last 15 mins, remove the paper and put back in the oven uncovered, to brown. After cooking, remove the meat and place in a warmed dish to rest. Make the sauce with the vegetables in the pan by straining off excess fat before adding more water if necessary together with 1tbsp of creamed coconut. Strain if you like, but I prefer not to, as you need all the goodness and crunchiness from the vegetables. Thicken sauce if necessary. Transfer beef to a carving board and cut into thick slices. Spoon over the sauce/vegetables and serve. Don't forget your roast potatoes!

Good Lord! How can anyone not like this, I wonder?

GREEN CURRY
NINA G'S STYLE

A chef at a hotel in Krabi, southern Thailand gave this recipe to me during a visit there. We enjoyed the wonderful curry meal so much, I plucked up the courage to ask her for the ingredients and she kindly obliged. I am using fish instead of chicken breasts, however. I find King fish firm when cooked and inexpensive to buy. Though I am using King fish, (which can be found in African and Asian supermarkets, vacuum packed), it does not have too much of a fishy odour as it absorbs all the flavours in the sauce. I have used basil leaves to complete my dish, to add intensity and flavour. Join me in this mouth-watering aromatic curry – prepared Nina G style!

Ingredients:

400g King fish cut into little cubes
2tbsp vegetable oil
2tbsp green curry paste
400 ml coconut milk
100 ml warm water
100g African garden eggs cut into wedges
3tbsp fish sauce
50g fresh basil (break into small pieces)
1tsp sugar

Empty milk into saucepan and add green paste. Stir on low heat to mix. Add the remainder of the ingredients (with the exception of the basil leaves) and simmer for 5/6 mins for fish to cook. Check fish is cooked to your satisfaction. Season with basil leaves and cook for a further minute before removing from heat. Your green curry is now ready to be served with plain white rice.

NB: *if fish is not to your liking, substitute chicken pieces, shrimp or any other kind of seafood.*

EGUSI GOULASH

Egusi seeds are flat, protein-rich seeds, which are ground and used to prepare the very popular Nigerian Egusi soup. Egusi is derived from a specific type of melon found in Africa. The seeds of the melon are dried and ground into a coarse powder. You can purchase egusi from African and Indian supermarkets. Although delicious by itself, Egusi soup is usually used as an accompaniment when eating Fufu. Fufu is another staple food of West Africa. To enjoy fufu the traditional way, you eat it with your hands licking your fingers in the process! Forget about the knives and forks! In this recipe, however, I am foregoing the Fufu and combining the Egusi with an eastern European-influenced goulash dish plus a hint of South-East Asia to boot!

Ingredients:

500g stewing beef cut into small cubes
1tbsp palm oil
2tbsp vegetable oil
1 cube beef stock dissolved into 200ml warm water
1 small tin of chopped tomatoes
1 medium onion, peeled and chopped
1tsp tomato puree
125g chestnut mushrooms
500g baby spinach (use frozen to save time)
1tbsp-dried crayfish
4tbsp ground egusi
1tsp chilli powder (optional)

Heat oil and add the meat together with the onion. Cook on medium heat for 5 mins, and then add the stock, mushrooms, tomato puree, crayfish and chilli powder (if required). Simmer for about 20/25 mins stirring. At this stage add the spinach together with the egusi and simmer for a further 10 mins. Check seasoning is to your taste.

This is delicious served with rice or boiled yam.

SUYA

(This is the Nigerian version of satay, shish kebab or
tikka dishes – roasted meat on a skewer!)

Suya is traditional street food cooked by roadside vendors and it
originated from Northern Nigeria by people from the small town of
Suya. It is very cheap and typically served with roasted or barbecued
plantain – you can also enjoy it with green salad. (If you don't fancy
meat, use fish or chicken instead). To fully appreciate Suya it should
be eaten with friends *al fresco*. It is best to marinate the meat for
24hrs (or at least a minimum of a couple of hours) to allow infusion
and tenderising of the meat. You can buy the Suya powder from
African or Indian shops, but if none is available in your area, Masala
barbeque spice powder or curry paste will suffice with a sprinkle of
lemon juice. To quench your thirst after eating Suya, what you need
is a very cold drink. Traditionally, we drink palm wine to wash the
food down. Unfortunately, the real palm wine cannot be obtained in
this country, so the nearest alternative is a very cold cider. And as to
how palm wine is obtained: easy peasy! Climb the palm tree (it must
be the wine producing palm, as there are several varieties), attach
gourds to the top of the tree where there is the virgin growth. The dew
and the juices will drip into the container. Incidentally, the container
should be left for a couple of days for enough wine to be collected
and served. Cheers!

Ingredients:

500g beef sirloin or topside
Juice of 1 large or 2 small lemons,
2tbsp Suya seasoning if you're able to lay your hands on it –
otherwise 2tbsp Masala barbeque spice powder or curry paste.
1tbsp peanut butter
1tbsp coriander seeds, crushed
2tbsp vegetable oil
1 large red onion, peeled and cut into thin rings

Get your butcher to slice the beef into thin flat strips or do it yourself,
using a sharp kitchen knife. Mix all the ingredients; marinate for a

couple of hours or if cooking the same day, ensure you marinate first thing in the morning and cover in cling film. Lay flat on an oiled baking tray or use individual skewers. Grill or barbeque the meat, on each side for a few minutes to taste. When cooked, serve with green salad leaves laced with the thinly sliced red onion rings. If you fancy extra filling, serve with barbecued plantain. Yum! Instantly reminds me of home.

To prepare plantain: don't peel! Stab all over with a fork, cut in half and place on a grill or barbecue. Turn occasionally until cooked right through. It shouldn't take more than 15/20 mins. The end result is a blackened looking plantain,; simply peel and add some butter, seasoned with a little salt if you prefer and serve.

SAUSAGE KEBABS

As I am trying to produce meals as economically as possible, instead of using more expensive cuts of meat for this recipe, I am using sausages, with a touch of spiciness added to it. It makes sense however, to use at least mid-priced sausages to ensure a decent meat content as the very basic varieties contain lots of fillers such as rusk and have a much higher fat content also. To be avoided whenever possible. This dish goes well served with coconut rice as a main meal and for a light supper, seasoned salad – really scrumptious!

Ingredients:

8 beef or pork sausages – cut about 3cm thick (you should have about 4 cuts from each sausage)
8 shallots, peeled, whole or one large red onion, cut into wedges
8 medium tomatoes, cut in half
1tbsp white wine vinegar
1tsp garlic granules
1tbsp soy sauce
2tbsp tomato ketchup
2tbsp running honey
1tsp chilli flakes
16 button mushrooms, washed and dried

Pre-heat the grill
You'll need 8 wooden kebab sticks or skewers soaked in water to stop them from burning.

In a mixing bowl, add the tomato ketchup, soy sauce, white wine vinegar, garlic granules, honey and chilli flakes and mix together before setting aside. Now pierce the meat and vegetables on to the skewers. Liberally brush the sauce all over the kebabs and put side by side in a foil-lined tin. Place under the grill, turning occasionally, whilst basting until the vegetables have blackened slightly and sausage pieces are properly cooked. By now there should be some juices from the vegetables and sausages in the baking tin. Empty this into the kebab sauce, mix well, warm through and pour over the cooked kebabs. Serve on a bed of coconut rice or some salad if you prefer.

NB: thicken the sauce with corn flour if required.

PLANTAIN MOUSSAKA

This is my version of the classic Greek dish, moussaka, using African ingredients, instead of aubergines. Very uncomplicated, and following the same principle as its Greek counterpart – you simply can't go wrong. As I've already mentioned, plantain is very popular in African cuisine and is extremely versatile. It can be boiled, fried, baked, roasted you name it - you can even make them into plantain balls!

Ingredients:

350g minced beef
2 ripe but firm plantains (peel and cut plantain in half, then slice lengthways thinly)
1 large onion, peeled and chopped
3 cloves garlic, peeled and chopped
1 thumb-sized ginger, peeled and chopped
1 small tin chopped tomatoes
300g baby spinach
1 chicken stock, dissolved in 100ml of warm water
100g Philadelphia (or other soft) cheese
50g fresh coriander, chopped (reserve some for garnishing)
100g Parmesan or mature Cheddar cheese, grated

Heat oven: 200°C/400°F/Gas mark 5

First prepare the spinach – empty the packet into a saucepan and pour boiling water over it, leave for 5 mins then squeeze out excess water, or use a frozen version.

Heat the oil and add the ginger, fry for 1 min, followed by the onions and garlic for a further 1 min. Then add the mince and cook for a further 5 mins until it resembles a kind of brown crumble. Now add the tomatoes, coriander and stock and cook for 5 mins, before adding the Philadelphia cheese. Stir well and check the seasoning.

Cover the base of a ceramic dish with half the sauce, top with the sliced plantain, followed by the spinach, then the remainder of the sauce. Spread the cheese evenly over the top of the moussaka and bake for 15/20 mins or until slightly brown on top. Serve immediately.

NB: this is a complete meal in itself, but if you require an accompaniment, a simple bowl of mixed, green salad should suffice.

COCONUT RICE

When it comes to rice, I am sure you'll all agree that some extra va-va-voom is needed! I am fed up with eating plain rice all the time. So, I have decided to inject some coconut passion combined with a dash of oriental zing into my rice recipe. Kaffir leaves are from the Kaffir lime, and are native to South East Asia. Both the fruit and the leaves are used in their cuisine. Buy them from Asian or Chinese grocery shops. Be warned –you may just fall in love with this dish!

Ingredients:

450g long grain rice
2 Kaffir leaves
200ml coconut milk
2 cardamom pods, crushed (optional)
½ tsp salt
1tsp butter or cooking oil

Boil the water in a large pan, add the rice and let it cook rapidly for a couple of minutes. Remove from heat, rinse off the starchy water under cold tap, drain, and then add the coconut milk, salt, Kaffir leaves and cardamom pods. Bring to boil, then reduce to a medium heat and cook until the liquid has been absorbed and rice is almost tender. Remove from heat and with the lid on, leave to cook in its own heat for another 10 mins. Remove Kaffir leaves, fluff up and serve.

PLAIN BOILED RICE

If you're learning to knit and you keep dropping a stitch, you'll never be able to cook rice properly. We all think it's simple to cook rice, but I can assure you it is not. There is a definite knack involved to achieving perfect rice. As for my poor husband, whenever he decides to do the cooking, you might guess what I end up getting: a thick lumpy mass like rice pudding! Poor devil - he does try!

Here's how I prepare mine, the proper way - hopefully, it'll catch on!

You need just a cup of rice, a pinch of salt and water.

In a large saucepan of boiling water, add the rice. Boil rapidly for about 10 mins stirring. Take off heat, empty the rice into a sieve and put under cold running tap, stirring, to remove the excess starch. Put the rice back in the saucepan and after adding a little salt and 100ml of cold water, place on the heat once again. Bring to the boil rapidly for about 10 mins and then simmer for a further 5 mins or until the water has been fully absorbed. Check the rice is tender. Turn off the heat and with the lid on, let it cook in its own heat for another 5 mins. This should ensure the rice to be completely separated and fluffy.

You see - I told you it was easy!

QUINOA RISSOTTO

A friend of mine, who is a real foodie, prepared a salad dish which she garnished with cooked quinoa and believe it or not, I got hooked! Pronounced KEEN-WAH, this whole grain, originating from South America was not widely used or known about until very recently. Now, you are starting to see it on supermarket shelves and included in restaurant menus. And rightly so - it is full of goodness, being an excellent source of protein and amino acids. It is a perfect substitute for people who have problems digesting wheat, as quinoa does not contain gluten. It provides the vegetarians among us with a wonderfully healthy alternative source of protein. However, I hope all will enjoy my simple and appetising take on risotto with a touch of China!

Ingredients:

200g quinoa,
1 white Chinese radish (also called daikon or mooli), peeled and chopped into small cubes

1 tin vegetable soup (400g)
1 medium sized onion, peeled and chopped
2 garlic cloves, peeled and pressed
2tbsp vegetable oil
100g chorizo, cut in half (optional) or use sweet red pepper instead
3 Chinese Kaffir leaves - if you can't find these, use bay leaves instead
2 bunches of bok choi (just tail) and chop finely including the crunchy stems
1tsp chilli (optional)
100g grated cheese – Parmesan or Cheddar
Chilli flakes for garnishing

In one saucepan, boil 500ml water, and add the quinoa. Bring to the boil then simmer for about 15 mins, stirring intermittently. The water should be fully absorbed by then and the quinoa is cooked (check it is tender). In the meantime, in a different heavy, thick-based pan, gently heat the oil, add the onion and garlic and stir for a couple of minutes, followed by the kaffir or bay leaves for a further 2 mins. Stir in the soup, check seasoning, and simmer for 5 mins. Add the cooked quinoa, chilli flakes, chorizo, chopped bok choi and radishes, stir well to blend and simmer for a further 5 mins. Remove from heat and with the lid on, leave to cook in its own heat for a further 5 mins. Again check seasoning before serving. Garnish with some chilli flakes if you prefer.

SAUSAGES COOKED WITH CABBAGE LEAVES

This is a recipe I have devised with kids in mind. It is so easy for busy mothers to prepare and will definitely appeal to children who don't like vegetables. The tomato and herb sauce is sold in all supermarkets.

8 sausages (preferably beef)
2 medium onions, chopped
3 cloves garlic, chopped
1 small cabbage (Savoy is best)
1 tbsp olive or vegetable oil
1 tbsp white wine and cream sauce
1 tin tomato and herb sauce - bought
1 tsp all-purpose savoury seasoning
2 cardamom pods, crushed
50ml warm water
Salt and coarse black pepper

Remove the hard outer leaves of the cabbage, wash, take out the core and chop into pieces. In a large pan, gently fry the chopped onions and crushed garlic, on a medium heat for 3 mins. Add the rest of the ingredients together with the water. Cover and cook for 15 mins on low flame. Check seasoning. Add a little more water if necessary. Serve with seasoned mashed potato.

CARROT PASTA BAKE

This is a very simple yet tasty pasta dish. I have been able to achieve its simplicity and cheapness by using mainly staple store cupboard ingredients. The only purchase here is the bacon and mature cheddar cheese – and veggies of course won't need the bacon anyway.

Ingredients:

225g penne pasta
200g streaky bacon, chopped
230g tinned chopped tomatoes
1 medium onion, peeled and chopped
2 large carrots, peeled and grated
1 sweet red pepper, deseeded and chopped
3 garlic cloves, peeled and pressed
1tbsp crème fraîche
200g Parmesan or Cheddar grated
2tbsp vegetable oil
Salt and pepper

Heat oven: 200°C/400°F/Gas mark 6

Boil pasta according to instructions (adding a little salt to the water) until tender and drain. Set aside and keep warm.

In a different saucepan, heat oil and add the onion, garlic and bacon and fry for 2 mins. Then add the tomatoes and cook on a low heat for about 5 mins. Now add the remainder of the ingredients (excluding the Parmesan and pasta). Simmer for 5 mins. Check seasoning. Empty the penne into the sauce, stir thoroughly and then transfer into an ovenproof dish. Top with the cheese and bake for 15/20 mins until golden brown.

Serve with crispy cabbage or salad.

STUFFED TOMATOES WITH MINCED BEEF

This is stuffed tomatoes with a difference. Very simple to prepare, not much fuss and full of goodness.

Ingredients:

440g minced beef
4 beef tomatoes
1 medium onion, peeled and chopped
2 garlic cloves, peeled and pressed
1tbsp soy sauce
50g coriander
1tsp all-purpose savouring seasoning
Salt and pepper

Heat oven: 200°C/400°F/Gas mark 5

Slice off the top of the tomatoes and scoop out flesh, liquidise and reserve. In a mixing bowl, empty the minced beef together with the remainder of the ingredients, mix well with your hands (I like to feel!). Fill each tomato with the mince and press down firmly until level. Place the sliced tops back on the tomatoes, resembling a hat. Line a baking tin with foil and grease with some oil. Bake for about 20/25 mins until cooked and slightly brown round the edges of the tomatoes. After 25 mins, if there is any juice in the roasting tin, tip this into whatever gravy you are making separately together with the liquidised tomato pulp and simmer for a couple of minutes. Again, check seasoning and serve with vegetables of your choice and seasoned mash.

NINA G'S MUSSELS SPECIAL

As you know, the best time to enjoy mussels is during the winter months when they are plentiful – so make the most of it! This is my version of finger-licking mussels in tomato sauce, easy and very tasty – enjoy!

1.5kg mussels, soaked and cleaned
1 medium onion, peeled and chopped
2 chillies deseeded and chopped
4 cloves garlic, peeled and crushed
1 tin tomato and herb sauce (from supermarkets)
3tbsp white wine/cream sauce
1 chicken stock dissolved in 600ml of warm water
100g bunch of basil (reserve some for garnishing)
Salt and fresh black pepper
1tbsp corn flour

Cook mussels in boiling water for 5/6 mins or until open – discard any unopened mussels. Drain in a colander and keep warm.

The sauce:

Sauté the chopped onion and garlic then add the remainder of the ingredients and simmer for 10 mins. Thicken the sauce with corn flour. Empty mussels into the sauce, stir well and check seasoning. Serve on warmed plates and garnish with remainder of basil leaves.

Serve with warm crusty bread or a bowl of chips for a tasty main meal.

NINA G'S MUSSELS SPECIAL –IN TOMATOES AND CIDER

Another Version….

If you fancy something with a very different kick, try this!

Ingredients:
1.5kg mussels, soaked and cleaned
1 medium onion, chopped
4 cloves garlic, peeled and chopped
4 tomatoes, skinned, and cut into wedges
2tbsp white wine/cream sauce
250ml dry cider
1 chicken stock dissolved in 300ml warn water
50g coriander, chopped (reserve some for garnishing)
Freshly ground black pepper

Cook mussels in boiling water for 5/6 mins or until open – discard all unopened mussels. Drain in a colander and keep warm.

The sauce:

Sauté the chopped onion, garlic and tomatoes for 5 mins. Then add the remainder of ingredients and simmer for a further 10 mins. Season to taste. Thicken sauce if you find the consistency is a bit light. Empty the mussels into the sauce and stir well thoroughly . Garnish with remainder of coriander leaves and serve immediately.

NINA G'S CURRY SAUCE MUSSELS SPECIAL

Having devised the mussels in cider and tomato sauce, I decided I wanted to try something much more intense. I mean the kind of intensity you have when you're about to fall in love. Another finger-licking affair!

Ingredients:
1.5kg mussels, soaked and cleaned
1 medium onion, peeled and chopped
4 garlic cloves, peeled and crushed
3tbsp olive or vegetable
2tbsp curry sauce
4 tomatoes, skinned and chopped
3tbsp white wine and cream sauce
1 chicken stock dissolved in 500ml of warm water
50g basil or coriander
Salt and pepper

Cook mussels in boiling water for 5/6 mins or until open – discard all unopened mussels. Drain in a colander and keep warm.

Sauté the chopped onion, garlic and tomatoes for 5 mins. Add the remainder of the ingredients and simmer for a further 10 mins. Season to taste. Thicken sauce if consistency is too light. Tip the mussels into the sauce and stir well. Serve immediately, garnished with remainder of coriander or basil leaves.

SALTED COD PIE WITH PALM OIL

Cod is the favourite fish in Nigeria. Whenever a recipe calls for fish, it's bound to be cod. Typically, it is used in soups and broths, but with this recipe, I have tried to westernise things by making a pie with it. Enjoy this hearty fish pie with an African twist!

Ingredients:

500g salt cod
2 medium potatoes
500g pumpkin, peeled and cubes
1 medium onion, peeled and chopped
2 garlic cloves, peeled and crushed
1tbsp palm oil
1tbsp vegetable oil
2 green chillies, deseeded and chopped
4 tomatoes, skinned and chopped
2tbsp white wine and cream sauce
Milk and butter

Pour boiling water over the cod and leave to de-salt for a minimum of two hours, preferably longer, changing the water intermittently, or after 24 hours if possible. Take out of the water and remove the bones and skin, then cut the flesh into small pieces.

Meanwhile, boil the potatoes and pumpkin until tender, drain and mash with milk and butter (to taste) and keep warm. Fry the garlic, onion, tomatoes and chillies for a couple of minutes then add the cod and remainder of the ingredients simmering for a further 5 minutes. Check seasoning before emptying the contents into an ovenproof dish. Spread the mash evenly on top of the cod mixture, brush with a little melted butter and bake for 15 mins until golden brown. Serve with green salad.

GRAVY-PASTED ROAST CHICKEN

Once, while looking through the ingredients in my kitchen in typical fashion, my thoughts turned to different ways one could use gravy granules. The end product was the idea of using them as a paste to coat chicken. I tried this first with chicken legs, and it was very rewarding. This gave me the confidence to try something bigger – hence a whole roasted chicken. The recipe is so straightforward and the end result was fantastic. Why not give it a try – you'll be amazed at the results!

Ingredients:

1 chicken, approximately1.4kg
4 tbsp olive oil
1tsp garlic granules
3tbsp gravy granules (you can decide the flavour), mixed into a
smooth paste with garlic granules (not runny)
2tbsp breadcrumbs
1 packet stuffing (sage and onion or other)

Heat oven: 190°C/375°F/Gas mark 4

Wash chicken and pat dry. Stuff the neck and bottom with stuffing. Slash across each thigh about 2 or 3 times. Now stab the chicken all over with a fork so that the seasoning will penetrate the flesh. Then rub the gravy paste all over the chicken with a cooking brush, paying particular attention to the cavity and the slashed thighs. Now sprinkle the breadcrumbs all over, place on a wire rack in the roasting tin, and put in the oven, basting intermittently. After 45 mins or thereabouts, you should see a crispy texture start to form on the breast area. Before turning the chicken over, empty the juice into a saucepan (part of the gravy juice) and brush some more paste onto the chicken and return to the oven. Cook for another 1hour 15 mins basting at regular intervals. Before removing from oven check chicken is cooked properly and that the juice is running clear. Rest chicken before serving with your favourite vegetables.

SWEET POTATO & CHICKEN CROQUETTES

Now you've enjoyed the roast chicken, time to make good use of the leftover meat on the bones. Cut away all the pieces of meat on the chicken. If you're lucky, you should be able to prise about 200 grams of chicken pieces from the carcass.

Ingredients:

200g chicken pieces, minced very fine
1 medium sized sweet potato, peeled and cubed
1 medium onion, peeled and chopped
1 medium red pepper, deseeded and chopped
1tsp paprika
50g butter
2 eggs, beaten
Vegetable oil for frying
Salt and coarse black pepper

Boil potatoes with a pinch of salt added to the boiling water. They shouldn't take more than 15 mins to cook (but do check that they are tender). Drain, add the butter and mash. Add the chicken and the remainder of the ingredients (not salt as yet). Mix thoroughly. Check seasoning by adding a little salt if needed. Roll out on a floured board. Shape into the size of small sausages. Fry in hot fat for about 5 mins, before draining on kitchen paper and serve with salad.

COCONUT MILK RISOTTO
WITH CORNED BEEF

Coconut milk is very versatile and can be used in most kinds of cooking. Where the recipe calls for fresh milk, try coconut milk instead. For a bit of oriental flavour, why not add it to deserts such as rice and bread puddings, pancakes, etc.

Having said that, here I have chosen to prepare this main course with coconut milk and corned beef. Corned beef is one of my mother's favourite meats, because you can prepare any kind of meaty dish with corned beef and believe it or not, it's full of flavour. When my parents lived in Fernando Po (now called Bioko), in Equatorial Guinea and because fresh meat was very scarce in the 1950's, she prepared most meals with corned beef to make up for the loss of available protein.

Ingredients:

375g risotto rice
350g chestnut mushrooms
2 cubes chicken stock dissolved in 600ml warm water
1tbsp vegetable oil
2 garlic cloves, peeled and chopped
1 thumb-sized fresh ginger, chopped
100ml coconut milk
50g coriander chopped including stalk (reserve some leaves for garnishing)
1 medium onion, peeled and chopped
340g corned beef (cut in half and keep the other half for garnishing)
200g tomatoes, skinned and chopped
Salt and coarse pepper

Heat the oil and fry the onion, garlic and ginger for 1 minute. Then add the chopped tomatoes and stir for another minute before adding the stock, rice, mushrooms and coriander, stirring continuously. Adjust the heat to medium on your stove. Continue stirring. You are now halfway through cooking time. Add the coconut milk, half the corned beef and carry on stirring intermittently until the liquid is absorbed but still moist. Check seasoning and add a little water if necessary. Serve garnished with the remaining corned beef, coriander and coarse black pepper.

CRAB MEAT WITH PORK

Before protesting that this sounds "yuk", bear with me here. Keep an open mind and I assure you, once you have tried it, you'll be hooked by how tasty this dish is.

Ingredients:

500g pork, cubed, seasoned with salt and pepper and coated in some corn flour to seal
2 small tins crab meat in brine
4 tomatoes, skinned and chopped
1 onion, peeled and chopped
3 cloves garlic, peeled and crushed
2tbsp olive or vegetable oil
1tbsp white wine and cream sauce
Pinch of salt and coarse black pepper
1tsp cayenne pepper
1 chicken stock dissolved in 500ml of warm water.
50g sage or basil

Fry pork on medium heat to seal for about 3/4 mins. and stir well. Add the onion, garlic, tomatoes and cayenne pepper and cook for a further 3/5 mins. Then, add the crabmeat contents together with the stock. Cover with a lid, bring to the boil and simmer on low heat for about 20 mins or until liquid has slightly evaporated and pork is cooked. Before you take off the heat check that the pork is tender, then add fresh sage or basil, rest for 5 mins, and stir again. Serve with new potatoes or mash.

PORK WITH CHINESE LEAVES

Another pork dish, this one with Chinese leaves, which work very well with the meat. If you're having difficulty getting hold of Chinese leaves, pointed green cabbage will suffice.

Ingredients:

500g pork meat, cubed, seasoned and coated with corn flour.
1 bunch Chinese leaves, sliced thinly
2 medium onions, peeled and chopped
2 cloves garlic, peeled and crushed
4 tomatoes, quartered
2tbsp white wine and cream or herb sauce
1tsp tomato purée
500ml chicken stock,
1tsp paprika pepper
1tbsp vegetable oil

Fry the pork on a medium heat to seal for about 3/4 mins and stir well. Add the onions, garlic, tomatoes and paprika pepper and cook for a further 3/5 mins. Then, add the remaining ingredients together with the stock. Cover with a lid, bring to the boil and simmer on low heat for about 20 mins or until liquid has slightly evaporated and the pork is cooked. Before you take off heat check that the pork is tender. Meanwhile, thinly slice the Chinese leaves and add. Mix and let cook on medium heat for 3 mins leaving the leaves still crunchy. Check seasoning. Serve with plain white or brown rice.

CHICKEN IN DRY CIDER

In this recipe, you will see that I have used lemon juice to marinate the chicken, as I find it firms the meat before cooking.

Ingredients:

4 pieces chicken breasts
2tbsp olive oil
4 smoked streaky bacon rashers, cut into pieces
200ml dry cider
1 medium onion, peeled and chopped
3 cloves garlic, peeled and crushed
2 tbsp white wine and cream sauce
50g coriander chopped and extra to garnish
3 tomatoes, skinned and chopped
Salt and black coarse pepper
1tbsp lemon juice
1tbsp tomato puree

Season the chicken pieces in salt, pepper and lemon juice and rest for 10 mins. Heat oil and fry chicken on medium heat, turning frequently until cooked and juice running clear and well browned. Remove and keep warm.

Sauce:
In a large pan, fry the onion and garlic for 2/3 mins on medium heat. Add bacon and tomatoes and cook for a further 3 mins. Then add the cider, white wine and cream sauce, tomato puree and chopped coriander. Bring to the boil and then simmer gently on a low heat, stirring occasionally for a further 5/6 mins. Check seasoning and add a little salt if required. If sauce has reduced too much, add a little water to improve the consistency.

Serve chicken cut diagonally, spoon over the sauce and garnish with the remaining coriander. The sauce is brilliant with boiled yam.

BRAISED OXTAIL IN FIORENTINO SAUCE

Oxtail was once regarded as the "poor man's food" but not any more. It requires very slow cooking to capture the full flavour of the tail. To improve the depth of flavour even more, cook the day before. If you have difficulty obtaining oxtail, you can substitute a couple of lamb shanks, cut in large chunks and they will do the trick.

Ingredients:

1 small oxtail, cut into 3cm thick
1 medium sized onion, peeled and chopped
2 cloves garlic, peeled and crushed
6 whole cherry tomatoes,
50g fresh rosemary, chopped
400g of frozen mixed vegetables
200g button mushrooms
1tbsp tomato puree
2tbsp cooking oil
2 beef stock cubes, made with 3 pints of water
1 small tub fresh Fiorentino sauce (bought from supermarket)
Salt and black pepper
2 tbsp corn flour or ordinary baking flour

Preheat oven to 175°/350°F/Gas mark 4.

Trim the fat off the meat. Rub the salt, pepper and flour into meat and fry gently for about 5 mins on medium heat, turning occasionally. Then add onion, garlic, cherry tomatoes, mushrooms and corn flour, and cook for a further 10 mins on a low heat, stirring occasionally. Add the stock liquid, frozen mixed vegetables, Fiorentino sauce, tomato puree and chopped rosemary and bring to the boil for about 5 mins. Empty the contents into a casserole dish and slow cook in the oven for 3½ hrs or until meat is tender and falling off the bone. Season to taste, skimming off excess fat. Serve with mashed potatoes.

NB: gradually and slowly enjoy sucking the juices from the bone after you've devoured it of its meat!

OKRA, AFRICAN GARDEN EGG, BACON
AND PLANTAIN SALAD

I have prepared this menu with some typical Nigerian ingredients, in the hope that it will appeal to a western palate. In these health and weight-conscious times, it is difficult for Nigerian cuisine to break through to a wider, international audience, as it comprises mainly carbohydrates. Another drawback is the difficulty one encounters in finding the right ingredients to prepare something that is agreeable to all.

Therefore, I have selected three easily obtainable ingredients in the west and shall give you a short summary as to how they are used in my country.

OKRA: This is a vegetable originating from tropical climates. It is used mostly in Nigerian and Indian cooking. The leaves on the okra plant are used to prepare different kinds of vegetable broth in Nigeria. To enjoy okra, you've got to like its velvety texture. It is an acquired taste. In Nigeria, the young okra is dried in the sun for a couple of days  and used to thicken sauces. My research tells me that okra is a good source of plant protein.

GARDEN EGGS: They come from the aubergine family. In Nigeria they are served raw, i.e. cut into wedges and served with hot pepper paste to welcome guests and washed down with palm wine. Garden eggs can be found in African or Indian shops in areas with a large Afro-Caribbean and Asian population.

PLANTAIN: Much bigger than bananas but derived from the same family, this is now very easy to come by. Again, you will find it in Afro-Caribbean and Indian shops or if you are lucky enough, some of the big supermarkets. But from my own experience, your best bet is Afro-Caribbean or Indian stores. If you buy green plantain, it is better to boil it and serve with mild or hot tomato sauce – spinach works really well with it. If on the other hand, you buy ripe plantain (which is what I have used in this recipe) they should be bright yellow and firm.

Ingredients:

6 medium sized okra, tail only (don't top it), cut lengthways, deseed, cut in half then toss in flour.
2 garden eggs, cut into small wedges
6 rashers smoked bacon, cut into pieces
2 medium ripe plantains, remove skin like a banana, cut in half and slice lengthways thinly about 1cm thick
1 small onion, chopped
2 garlic cloves, chopped
2 tbsp vegetable or sunflower oil
1tsp all-purpose savoury seasoning
Salt and pepper

Heat the oil and fry the okra, onion and garlic for a couple of minutes, stirring continuously. Then add the garden eggs and bacon and continue stirring on a medium heat to bind. Check the seasoning, adding salt and pepper to taste. This should take no more than 6 mins. Keep warm.

To fry plantain: cut as described above and season with a little salt. Heat enough oil and fry until they are medium brown on both sides. Remove from heat and drain on kitchen paper.

Arrange cooked plantain on individual plates, top with the prepared okra and garden egg sauce and serve.

Yum!

TUNA AND BAKED BEANS PARCEL

You might think this is a weird combination, but when you are playing around with ingredients, like I do, you are bound to end up with unusual results from time to time. It is so simple; you can prepare it with your eyes shut!

For this one, I simply combined some tinned tuna, with baked beans, chopped dried tomatoes and some chopped, fresh flat leaf parsley or coriander and voila!

Ingredients:

415g tuna in brine (reserve brine) – or salmon if preferred
415g baked beans, drain sauce
6 sun-dried tomatoes, chopped
20g fresh chopped parsley or coriander
50g butter, melted
8 filo pastry, sheets (25cm x 25cm)
Pinch dried chilli (optional)

Heat oven: 200°C/400°F/Gas mark 5

In a ceramic bowl, empty contents of the tuna (reserving the brine) or salmon. Then add the baked beans, sun dried tomatoes and parsley or coriander (reserving some chopped leaves for garnishing) and mix gently with a wooden spoon to blend.

Now have your filo pastry ready. A word of warning, the pastry can be a bit fiddly to handle, so you've got to be quick when pasting both sides with butter before it dries out.

Spread out two sheets per person onto a clean kitchen board, one on top of the other, (because they are too thin to use individually). Brush with melted butter on one side, then gently turn the pair over and brush on the other side. Spoon the mixture into the middle of the pastry, then fold together, picking up one tip and overlapping the other, i.e. like a small envelope, until all the edges are sealed. Brush again with any remaining butter to ensure that the parcels are sealed. Bake for about 15/20 mins or until golden brown

Cool and serve.

You might ask, having prepared the parcels, what do I serve them with? Well, in my case, I decided the answer lies with spaghetti or pasta.

Cook the spaghetti or pasta according to instructions and when cooked, drain. Mix 2 tbsp olive oil with the brine and the baked bean sauce together with 1 tbsp of green pesto, (bought in any supermarket), toss the boiled spaghetti in this mixture and serve as a side dish to the parcel. What could be easier?

BONELESS LAMB NECK FILLET

I got the idea of using cloves in this recipe during my travels to Zanzibar. I love the aroma it gives when combined with cardamom pods. The crushed cloves and cardamom work well with the lamb, which leaves the cooked meat very tender and succulent, and greatly helps to improve both flavour and texture. But to achieve this, the meat has to be marinated and covered with cling film and left for approximately 24hours. If this is not possible, a minimum couple of hours of marinating will be okay.

Ingredients:

4 lamb neck fillets
6 cloves
6 cardamom pods
2tbsp cooking oil
1 Maggi (or other) beef stock cube

Crush the cloves, cardamom pods, garlic and stock cube in a ceramic dish and mix with the oil. Stab the meat with a fork to enable the mixture to penetrate the meat. Now rub the mixture thoroughly all over the meat with your hands, cover with cling film and leave in the fridge overnight. Two hours before cooking remove from fridge and leave at room temperature.

It would help the cooking process if you use a heavy base frying pan. Now heat the pan and empty the marinated oil into it. Add the meat and fry on a medium heat for 2 to 4 mins on each side depending on the thickness and how rare you prefer your meat. If you like your meat well done, fry for a little bit longer. Rest for 5 mins and cut diagonally.

Serve on individual warmed dishes, with new potatoes and vegetables and some gravy drizzled over the top.

PORK CHOPS IN WHITE WINE VINEGAR

I have used vinegar in this recipe for a tart, savoury touch. You need something sharp and fruity to balance the heaviness of the pork.

Ingredients:

4 loin pork chops
1tbsp white wine vinegar
3 garlic cloves, peeled and crushed
300ml warm water for gravy
2tbsp white wine and cream sauce
2tbsp gravy granules
1tsp dried oregano
1tbsp vegetable oil

Heat oven: 190°C/375°F/Gas mark 5

In a ceramic bowl, mix the vinegar, oregano and crushed garlic with the oil and marinate the meat. Cover with cling film and leave for 2hrs.

Arrange the chops on a baking dish and scatter the crushed garlic on top of the pork together with the oil and bake for 20 mins. Check it is properly cooked, then remove from the oven, cover and rest.

On a slow heat, mix gravy granules with warm water and pour into the baking dish together with white wine and cream sauce. Keep stirring until the sauce thickens and if too light, add a little corn flour. Check seasoning. Remove from heat and serve.

STUFFED PORK CHOPS WITH SPINACH

I hope I start a trend by stuffing pork chops with spinach! As usual, this recipe was born out of experimentation and believe you me, it is brilliant. I am not saying so because I prepared it, but you only have to try it yourself to agree.
So, let's hit the road.

Ingredients:

4 pork chops, about 5cm thick
100g sage and onion stuffing (bought)
100g frozen, finely chopped spinach (bought)
1tsp minced garlic
1tsp all-purpose savoury seasoning
Salt and coarse pepper

Heat oven: 190°C/375°F/Gas mark 5

Prepare the meat by trimming off some excess fat. Prepare the packet stuffing according to instructions. Defrost the spinach and squeeze out any excess water. Mix the stuffing and spinach together well with a fork, then add the garlic and all-purpose seasoning.

To make the pocket: lay the pork chop flat on a clean surface, hold down the chop with your palm, then with a sharp knife, slit through the chop horizontally. Gently stuff each chop with the mix, season with salt and pepper. Rub some oil on the roasting tin and transfer the chops onto it. Cover with foil and bake for 45/50 mins. Remove the foil, empty any juice and then cook for a further 10 mins to allow browning of the meat.

Make gravy with pan juice and serve with mash and crispy sautéed cabbage.

Happy eating!

CHICKEN OR TURKEY COOKED IN CAJUN SPICE

This is a recipe from left-over Christmas chicken or turkey. Instead of currying your chicken or turkey, opt for something a little more subtle. Cajun spice will do the trick; it's mildly hot and gives the sauce an exotic, piquant flavour.

Ingredients:

Cut your chicken or turkey into small pieces, carefully removing the meat off the bones (allow 50g per person)
1tbsp Cajun spice
1 small pickled gherkin, cubed very small
300ml coconut milk
1 chicken stock cube, dissolved in 100ml warm water
1tsp turmeric
1 medium onion, peeled and chopped
4 large tomatoes, skinned and chopped (reserve some for garnishing)
50g coriander, chopped
1 thumb-sized ginger or ½ tsp dried ginger
2tbsp vegetable oil

Heat the oil and fry the onion and ginger. Then add the remaining ingredients, bring to the boil and simmer for 15 mins. Check seasoning and thicken with corn flour if necessary. Remove from heat and garnish with the remainder of the tomatoes.

Serving suggestion: works really well with white rice

CHICKEN IN PEANUT BUTTER SAUCE

This is another easy chicken recipe; just by adding peanut butter whilst cooking gives it a touch of oriental flavour without having to get all the ingredients to prepare a Thai chicken recipe.

Ingredients:

375kg chicken fillets cut into biteable sizes
1 chicken stock dissolved in 500ml warm water
3tbsp crunchy peanut butter
1 medium onion, peeled and chopped
3 garlic cloves, peeled and crushed
1tbsp tomato puree
1 thumb-sized ginger, chopped
1 medium red pepper, deseeded and chopped
1tbsp corn flour
2 tbsp vegetable oil

Prepare the chicken by rubbing the salt, pepper and corn flour into the meat, heat oil and fry quickly to seal. Add the pepper, onion, garlic and ginger and cook for a further 5 mins. Then add the stock, tomato puree and peanut butter. Bring to boil and simmer for 20/25 mins. Check seasoning - add salt and pepper if required. Thicken with corn flour if the consistency is a bit runny or if too dry, add a little water. Stir well, remove from heat and serve with boiled potatoes and vegetables.

This sauce also goes well with boiled rice.

CHICKEN BREASTS STUFFED WITH SAUSAGES

I made this recipe with leftover sausages in the fridge!

Ingredients:

4 chicken breasts
250g Lincolnshire sausages
50g basil, chopped - reserve some for garnishing
1 medium onion, peeled and chopped
8 medium tomatoes, skinned and cut into wedges
2tbsp white wine and cream sauce
2 garlic cloves, peeled and crushed
2tbsp vegetable or olive oil
150ml warm water
Salt and coarse black pepper

Heat oven: 190°C/375°F/Gas mark 5

Line an ovenproof dish with olive oil. Prepare the chicken breasts by rubbing them all over with some salt and pepper. Cut the sausages into small pieces, adding a handful of basil, to make it easier to stuff in the chicken. Make a small pocket lengthways in each chicken breast and fill it with sausage meat and hold together with toothpick. Baste chicken with some oil, place in the greased, ovenproof dish, cover with foil and cook for 30 mins. Remove the foil, add half the tomatoes and cook for a further 5 mins to brown. Remove and keep warm.

Sauce:
Fry onion, garlic and the remainder of tomatoes on gentle heat for about 5 mins. Add cream sauce, some basil, water, salt and pepper and simmer for about 5/6 mins, stirring intermittently until sauce thickens. Season to taste and garnish with remainder of basil.

Serve with boiled rice.

TOAD IN THE HOLE

I doubt if families prepare this old fashioned toad in the hole anymore. You rarely hear people mention it in their daily lives. When I arrived in this country in the 1960's, this was my favourite prepared by my then landlady. Unfortunately, she did not serve it with gravy but with tomato sauce, which I hated.

Ingredients:

8 beef or pork sausages
50g fresh rosemary
1 small onion, peeled and chopped finely
1 packet of batter mix

Heat oven: 190°C/375°F/Gas mark 5

Buy prepared batter from the supermarket to save time and follow instructions. Add the chopped onion and rosemary to the batter and use as below.

First of all prick the sausages and place them in a baking dish approximately 28cm x 20cm. Heat them in the oven to get rid of some of the fat for about 10 mins. Drain off the liquid and then pour the batter mix over the sausages. Return to the oven and cook for about 30 mins or until the batter has risen and is golden brown. Cut into portions of 2 sausages each and serve immediately with any crunchy vegetables of your choice with lots and lots of gravy.

CHINESE PORK SPARE RIBS
COOKED IN COCONUT CREAM and GOLDEN SYRUP

This is one of those finger-licking recipes for ribs to be enjoyed during the hot summer months. Don't be shy to tuck in by hand – that's part of the fun! An abundance of paper napkins would be of immense help, however...

Ingredients:

1.5kg Chinese style pork spare ribs
3tbsp golden syrup or honey
2tbsp tomato ketchup
60ml white wine vinegar
2tbsp Worcester sauce
4tbsp coconut milk
½ level tsp chilli pepper
2 garlic cloves, crushed
½ tsp salt (if needed)

Heat oven: 180°C/350°F/Gas mark 4

The only way to get the ribs moist and tender is to pre-boil them for about 15 mins. (Save the stock for making gravy).

Now mix all the above ingredients in a mixing bowl with a fork. Arrange the ribs in a baking tin, pour over the sauce, cover with foil and cook for 20 mins. Remove foil and drain any juice from the baking tin into a bowl. Brush the sauce on the ribs, increase oven heat, back into the oven and further bake for 15 mins brushing with sauce until brown all over.

Remove from oven, rest for about 10 mins. In warmed dishes, drizzle the remaining sauce all over the ribs. Serve accompanied by green salad, potato wedges and lastly some crusty bread to soak up any juices. (Thicken sauce with corn flour if necessary).

NINA'S FRIED SPAGHETTI WITH EGGS

The Chinese like their fried rice with eggs but I like my eggs with spaghetti! I have devised this recipe with children in mind. They'll love it! Though the ingredients are for 4 people, you can always increase or decrease the quantities to suit.

Ingredients:
450g spaghetti
2tbsp vegetable oil
4 firm ripe tomatoes, skinned, deseeded and cubed
6 bacon rashers, chopped
50g parsley, chopped (retain some for garnishing)
4 medium eggs
2tbsp white wine and cream sauce
2 medium sized onions, peeled and chopped
Salt and coarse black pepper
Cheese for garnishing

Boil the spaghetti according to the instructions on the packet (about 10 mins but check that it is done). Meanwhile, fry the onions and bacon until slightly brown but not burnt. As soon as the spaghetti is ready, drain and empty contents into the bacon and onion (remember the pan is on very low heat). Add the cream sauce (if you fancy some moistness, add a little water), tomatoes and parsley. Lastly, break the eggs onto the mixture, with a wooden spoon, stir rapidly for the ingredients to blend. Check seasoning. Serve garnished with some parsley together with the grated cheese.

KIDNEY WITH STREAKY BACON
COOKED IN SWEET CIDER

For whatever reason, kidneys seem to be eaten less and less, but I've devised a recipe, which, I hope, will excite your taste buds. Kidney is full of iron, which we need as sustenance to get us through our daily lives. Prepared with some fresh tomatoes, cider and whatever ingredients you fancy, should make the difference. Not only will it make an exciting meal for the family, it is very cheap and cheerful!

Ingredients:

250g lamb kidneys
4 medium tomatoes, skinned, deseeded and sliced
1 medium onion chopped
2 garlic cloves, peeled and crushed
250g smoked streaky bacon, cut into manageable pieces
2tbsp vegetable oil
350ml sweet cider or any cider will suffice
1tbsp white wine and cream sauce
50g coriander, chopped
1tbsp corn flour
Salt and coarse black pepper

Trim the fat and skin the kidneys. Cut in half, season with salt, pepper and corn flour to bind. Heat the oil and fry the kidneys for a couple of minutes to brown and seal, remove from the heat and set aside. Fry the bacon until fairly brown then add the onion and garlic, stirring continuously. Then add the cream sauce and cider and bring to the boil, then simmer for 10 mins. Now add the kidneys, coriander and chopped tomatoes and simmer for a further 5 mins for all the ingredients to blend. Check seasoning.

Garnish with the remaining coriander and serve with seasoned mashed potatoes.

SAUTÉED KIDNEYS

This is another quick and easy way of preparing kidneys. It's a doddle!

Ingredients:

250g lamb kidneys
2tbsp vegetable oil
2tbsp white wine and cream sauce
1tsp dry thyme
2tbsp Masala wine (optional)
Corn flour for binding
Salt and coarse ground black pepper

Trim the fat and skin the kidneys. Slice kidneys very thinly, season with salt and pepper and coat with the corn flour. Heat oil and cook quickly, tossing all the time for a couple of minutes. Reduce heat, add the remainder of the ingredients and cook for a further 5 mins. Check seasoning. Serve whilst hot with some potato wedges or as a light supper with green salad.

FISH CAKES WITH
TINNED SALMON

I am using tinned salmon for this fish recipe to cut cost. The end result is the same as if using fresh fish, but the only difference is the savings made to your weekly budget and that your purse is slightly heavier!

Ingredients:

418g x 2 tinned pink salmon in brine
50g butter
50g coriander or basil, chopped
1 egg, beaten
1 small sweet red pepper, deseeded and chopped
1 large potato, boiled and mashed with butter
1tbsp white wine and cream sauce
100g breadcrumbs
Vegetable oil for frying

Empty the fish into a ceramic mixing bowl (save the brine to use later). Add the remainder of the ingredients (excluding the egg), and mix well with a wooden spoon. Transfer the contents on to a wooden board covered in half the breadcrumbs. Flatten the mixture, then, using a small teacup as a cutter, cut out as many patty shapes as possible, about half centimetre thick. Coat all over with the other half of the egg, then the breadcrumbs and fry. Drain. Serve with crispy cabbage and sautéed potatoes.

NB: thicken brine with corn flour, adding pinch of salt and black pepper and drizzle over the fish cake.

FISH AND CHEESE PIE

This is a very simple, cheap and cheerful fish recipe that I have devised with cheese sauce from a packet.

Ingredients:

418g x 2 tinned pink salmon in brine
50g butter
50g coriander or basil, chopped
1 packet cheese sauce (prepare according to instructions on packet using the brine, if not enough, add more liquid)
1 whole lemon, cut into 4 wedges
2 hard boiled eggs, sliced
1 small gherkin, grated
Salt and coarse black pepper

In an oven-proof casserole dish, arrange the salmon in an even layer, then top with the boiled eggs and cubed gherkin. Pour the cheese sauce over the fish, and sprinkle with the salt and black pepper. Bake in a hot oven for 10/15 mins to brown on top. Serve with lemon wedge, potato wedges and peas.

CASSAVA CASSEROLE

Cassava is a root vegetable belonging to the same family as yam, sweet and ordinary potatoes. Widely grown and now consumed in Asia and the Caribbean - it was introduced to Asian countries by migrants. Cassava is a staple food in Nigeria, as well as India and the West Indies. Different nationalities prepare cassava in different ways, but the most common way of preparing cassava in Nigeria is after harvesting, the crop is peeled, grated and dried and then made into "garri".

Garri is served with a kind of vegetable broth containing either fish or beef. When the cassava is cut open, there is a woody string that runs down the middle of the cassava, which should be carefully carved out. To preserve its flavour and before transportation, the outer layer is commercially waxed.

Ingredients:

400g cassava, peeled and cubed
8 pork sausages, pricked and browned under a hot grill to remove

some fat, then cut in half
1tsp garam masala
1 onion, peeled and chopped
2 carrots, peeled and cubed
2 garlic cloves, peeled and crushed
4 bacon rashers cut into small pieces
1 chicken stock cube, dissolved in 250ml of warm water
2tbsp vegetable oil
50g coriander, chopped (reserve some for garnishing)
2tsp cayenne pepper
Salt and coarse black pepper

Sauté the onion and garlic, then add the bacon and cassava and simmer for about 3 mins, stirring continuously.. Add the liquid and the remainder of ingredients (excluding the cooked sausages) bring to boil, and then simmer for about 15 mins. Now add the sausages and simmer for a further 10 mins. Check the cassava is tender and the seasoning is just right for you.

Serve with green vegetables.

TENDERLOIN OF PORK
WITH OLIVE SAUCE

There are differences between loin pork and tenderloin pork, the latter being long and leaner with no fat or bone. Tenderloin pork, as the name implies, is tender, juicy and full of flavour. Pork loin roast is for roasting, though full of flavour as well, but it takes longer to prepare. Because of the richness of the pork, I have used olives to counteract this and also added some white wine vinegar.

Ingredients:

1kg tenderloin pork
1 small onion, peeled and chopped
8 green olives without stones, chopped
1tsp white wine vinegar
1tsp tomato purée
1tsp mixed herbs
1tsp mustard
100ml warm water
2 garlic cloves, peeled and crushed
2tbsp natural breadcrumbs
Salt and coarse black pepper
Butter for frying

Wrap the pork in some cling film and flatten the meat slightly. Combine the salt, pepper and breadcrumbs and rub all over the meat. Stand for 10 mins. Heat the butter and fry on a medium/low heat, basting intermittently. In total, it should not take more than 20 mins. Remove from the heat, wrap foil around meat and rest for a further 10 mins.

Sauce:

Fry the onion and garlic for a couple of minutes, then add the remainder of ingredients and stir for a further couple of minutes. Add water to the frying pan and scrape the entire residue from pan and empty contents into a saucepan. Bring to the boil and simmer for 5 mins. Cool and liquidise. Put sauce through a sieve. Place back on the heat, check seasoning and if needed, thicken with some corn flour. Cut the meat into 2cm thick slices and serve with the sauce.

Serve with broccoli and roast potatoes.

DESSERTS

PINEAPPLE FRITTERS

Finish off your dinner gatherings with this lovely light sweet. The addition of almond extract gives it that extra "oomph" and a delicate flavour to enhance the somewhat bland batter. If you buy fresh pineapple, allow to rest for a couple of days before using. As you know having travelled long distance, the poor devil is stressed and needs time to rest!

If using fresh pineapple, cut in rings around 2½cm thick, peel and remove the stalk. If using tinned pineapple, 2 each per person, as the tinned ones always seem very small.

4 pineapple rings – 2½cm thick (carefully carve out the stalk in the middle)
50ml ice water
50g plain flour
1 large egg (separate the white and the yolk; beat the egg white to stiffen)
2tsp almond extract
1tbsp sesame seeds
Vegetable oil for deep frying
Ice cream for accompaniment

Whisk the water and egg yolk in a bowl thoroughly, then slowly add the flour beating until smooth. Fold in the almond extract and let the mixture stand for 1hour before using - longer if time permits. Before using, fold in the egg white and mix well with a wooden spoon.

Coat the pineapple rings with the batter, and deep fry in hot oil. Drain in absorbent paper towel and serve topped with ice cream, cream or crème fraîche.

NB: for really good results, deep fry the fritters.

PEACHES IN RUM

Sorry folks, if you become legless, I hold my hands up! And for the kiddiewinks, I am terribly, terribly, sorry, this one is not for you.

Ingredients:
4 peaches
4tbsp rum
4tbsp castor sugar
Ice cream and some mint leaves for garnishing

Soak the peaches in boiling water for a couple of minutes. Cool and peel off skin, cut in half, twist and remove stone. Place in individual dessert or wine glasses, sprinkle with sugar and top with rum. Cover in cling film and leave in the fridge for a couple of hours. Serve, topped with ice cream and garnish with mint. If you have them, this also goes well with dessert biscuits.

NB: you can always buy rum flavouring from the supermarket if you haven't got the real stuff.

WHALLA MANGO PARCELS

My French is not too good and when I originally experimented with this recipe and mastered it, I said "whalla"! My husband pointed out that the French word for "that's it" is actually "voila", but the name stuck for this delightful and different desert.

One more point I would like to make is that you need to have your skates on when preparing the dessert because of the inclusion of the ice cream before it starts melting.

Ingredient:

1 large or 2 medium ripe mangoes
2tsp almond extract or any flavouring of your choice
8 sheets filo pastry (25cm x 25cm)
50g butter, melted
Ice cream – have already in the freezer compartment 4 separate scoops of ice cream, as you need them very hard before using.
Vegetable oil for deep-frying

Peel the mangoes and chop the flesh into tiny pieces. Add the almond extract stir and keep to one side.

Meanwhile, onto a clean kitchen board, spread out 2 sheets per person of the filo pastry,, one on top of the other. Brush with melted butter on one side of the pair, then gently turn over and brush on the other side. Spoon the mango mixture into the middle of the pastry and add the ice cream. Quickly fold the filo, picking up all 4 tips and form into the size of a tennis ball. Brush again with any remaining butter to ensure that it is all sealed.

It is advisable to use a deep fryer, if possible, for this recipe for good results.

Heat the oil and when slightly smoky, drop the thick side in first and within 2/3 mins, it should be brown and crispy all over.

Remove and serve immediately – just cutting through the pastry case you will see the ice cream oozing out as if slicing through Chicken Kiev.

Enjoy!

BAKED MANGO PUDDING

Another delicious mango recipe for you to enjoy. A reminder: always rest bought mangoes for a couple of days before use.

Ingredients:

2 ripe mangoes (firm)
2 medium eggs
2tbsp rum or gin
6 stale thick slices bread (trim off the crusts)
Butter (for spreading on bread)
2tbsp raisins
2tbsp castor sugar
300ml full cream milk
2tbsp clear honey

Peel the mangoes and slice. Arrange in a buttered oven proof dish and sprinkle a handful of raisins on the mangoes. Beat the eggs then add the milk, rum, and remaining raisins and stir in half of the sugar and set aside.

Butter the bread slices and dip each in the egg mixture and gently place on the prepared mangoes, buttered side up. Continue until the mangoes are completely covered with the soaked bread. Pour over any left over mixture. Sprinkle the top with the remainder of the sugar and raisins and drizzle the honey all over. Bake for 15/20 mins at 190°C, 375°F or gas mark 5, or until brown on top.

Serve immediately with ice cream or crème fraîche.

MANGO IN SWEET & SOUR CREAM
WITH DESICCATED COCONUT

This recipe calls for fresh ingredients; if you have any difficulty obtaining fresh mango, you can use peaches instead.

Ingredients:

1 large ripe mango, peeled and cubed
1tsp vanilla extract
1 small tub of soured cream
2tbsp golden syrup or honey
½ tsp coarse black pepper
2tbsp desiccated coconut

Mix mangoes, black pepper and honey in a ceramic bowl. Spoon the mixture into four ramekins, and top with soured cream and desiccated coconut and brown quickly under a hot grill (or you can use a blow torch) and serve.

IVY'S PUDDING

This is one of my daughter's favourites when she still lived at home. Now that she has flown the nest, she still comes back for more. A straightforward dessert using sweet eating apples

Ingredients:
8 stale thick sliced bread, crusts removed
4 pink lady apples or any sweet eating apples of your choice
1tsp cumin seeds
1tsp vanilla extract
50g butter
1 egg, whisked
2tbsp sesame seeds
1tbsp brown sugar
Clear honey for drizzling over pudding

Heat oven: 200°C/425°F/Gas mark 6

Peel, core and slice the apples and place in a bowl. Add cumin seeds and vanilla extract, cover with cling film and cook on high in a microwave for 8 mins. Mash roughly with a fork and set to one side. Meanwhile, butter the bread on one side only. Take one slice of bread, buttered side down, fill with prepared apple (about 1tbsp) in the middle of bread, then cover with another slice of bread, buttered side up. With a pastry brush, moisten the edges with the beaten egg; pinch the edges lightly to seal. Sprinkle the top with brown sugar, followed by the sesame seeds. Arrange on a buttered baking tray and cook for about 10/15 mins or until brown on top and crispy. Serve with your favourite ice cream.

PLUM SUMMER DESSERT

This is a dessert I enjoy serving after having Moussaka, because I find Moussaka in general to be a heavy meal. A simple and refreshing pudding when plums are in season. If plums are not available, use caramelised sweet apples with ice cream or crème fraîche.

Ingredients:

8 plums
1 tsp vanilla extract
4tbsp castor sugar
½ tsp cinnamon powder
Ice cream, single cream or crème fraîche for serving
Mint leaves for garnishing.

In a bowl, pour boiling water over the plums, cover and leave for 5 mins then peel.

Mix the vanilla extract, sugar and cinnamon powder together in a ceramic dish. Add the plums and cover with cling film. Place in the fridge and leave for 1hr or even longer. By now the plums should produce their own claret coloured juice. Drizzle the juice over the plums and garnish with mint leaves. Serve topped with ice cream, crème fraîche or single crème.

NB: this desert can be prepared a day before to allow fusion to take place.

PLUM PUDDING

If you have some leftover plums, this is a simple and delicious way of using them up.

Ingredients:

4 ripe plums, de-stoned and thinly sliced
50g butter
2 large or 3 medium eggs, separate yolk and white
4tbsp plain flour + ½ tsp baking powder (or 4tbsp self-raising flour)
½ tsp lemon juice, plus grated zest
4tbsp castor sugar
4tbsp crème fraîche
4tbsp clear honey
Icing sugar for dusting

Grease the four ramekins (size 85mm) with butter, line the bottom with the honey then with the sliced plums.

Beat the egg yolks and sugar together until creamy. Add lemon and zest and beat again lightly. Sieve in the flour and mix. Whisk the egg white until stiff and fold into the egg mixture. Spoon into the ramekins and level off. Arrange in a baking pan, pour boiling water round the ramekins (to about half way) and cook for 20/25 mins. Remove from the oven and when cool enough to handle, ease around the pudding with a sharp knife and tilt upside down onto a plate. Top with crème fraîche, dust with icing sugar and serve.

APPLE FOOL

This is a very simple recipe for the whole family. Very light to finish your meal if you've had a heavy main course.

Ingredients:

2 Pink lady or any sweet apples of your choice (you can use peaches instead having skinned and mashed them first)
30g icing sugar
1tbsp vanilla extract
1tbsp rum (optional)
3tsp gelatine or 2 gelatine leaves
125ml double cream
2 egg whites
1tbsp lemon juice

Peel and core the apples, then grate. Put into a muslin bag, sprinkle lemon juice all over (to avoid discoloration) and wait for 10 mins, squeezing out the excess juice. Dissolve the gelatine in 1tbsp of water over a bowl of boiling water, cool then pour over the apple. Whisk the cream with the sugar, rum and vanilla until it forms a peak. Whisk the egg whites until stiff. Gradually combine the mixture with apples until well blended. Fill four ramekins and leave in the fridge for a couple of hours to firm. Serve with dessert biscuits if you prefer or drizzle some caramelised sugar over for a bit of colour.

PINEAPPLE FLAN

This is a straightforward flan with pineapple to be enjoyed warm with custard. You can have it with ice cream if you prefer, either way, it is delicious.

Ingredients:

180g plain flour
1tsp baking powder
100g castor sugar
1tbsp brown Demerara sugar
1 large can of pineapple rings
1tsp almond extract
2 eggs
50g butter
1 tbsp desiccated coconut
Pinch of salt

Heat oven: 190°C/375°F/Gas mark 5

Mix the flour, baking powder and salt in a bowl. Make a well in the centre, crack in the eggs and mix with a fork until smooth. Then add the castor sugar and almond extract, mixing to a smooth paste. Finally, stir in the melted butter and mix.

Grease a 23cm baking dish, line the dish with the pineapple, then pour the batter over the fruit. Sprinkle with desiccated coconut followed by the Demerara sugar. Bake in the oven for about 30 mins, and it is ready when firm to the touch.

Cool, slice and serve with custard.

RICE AND BANANA PUDDING

I am sure we all love bananas and we should include them as part of our daily diet. Bananas are a staple fruit in Caribbean and African countries and are best eaten in the morning as they give us that extra energy at the start of the day. It is a shame that bananas are not grown in this country due to the weather, as we have to resort to importing them from hot climates. Because the storage temperature has had to be regulated in transit, the flavour is lost by the time it gets to its destination.

When purchasing bananas, make sure they have a firm yellowy colour (not soft) and the skin is not discoloured. If you are preparing any recipe that calls for the use of bananas, use the fruit straightaway after peeling as if it is exposed to air, this causes discolouration. To avoid this, always sprinkle with lemon juice.

Anyway, whatever the condition on arrival, it is full of sugar, starch and vitamins.

Enough of my preaching – let's prepare a little pudding, especially for kids – adults look away now or they can indulge as well.

Ingredients:

250g can of rice pudding (bought)
4 ramekins
3 small bananas (cut into rings)
4tbsp Demerara sugar
A handful of raisins
1tsp vanilla essence

Heat the grill:

Empty rice pudding into a bowl, add the raisins and vanilla essence, mix, then fill the ramekins halfway. Top with some bananas then finish off with the remainder of the rice pudding. Sprinkle sugar on top, place under a hot grill until it bubbles and turns brown. Leave in the fridge to firm then serve.

FLAMED BANANAS WITH RUM

This is an indulgent way to end a heavy lunch or dinner with friends!

(NB: I'm afraid, this is not for children, or alternatively, you can omit the rum)

Ingredients:

4 ripe firm bananas
50g butter
50g Demerara sugar
4tbsp rum
Ice cream of your choice
2tbsp lemon juice

Peel bananas and cut each diagonally in half. In a heavy frying pan, heat and melt the butter, add the sugar and continue stirring for about 3 mins or until slightly caramelised. (Don't let the sauce burn, as it'll be bitter). In goes the lemon juice next, and then the bananas, stirring all the time to coat the bananas for about 1 minute. Serve on individual plates, drizzling the rum over the bananas. Light with a match (averting your face) and wait until the flames die down before serving with ice cream.

Man this is good!

GRILLED PINEAPPLE WITH
HONEY/MINT/ICE CREAM

Pineapple is one of my favourite fruits. It is grown in Nigeria, my country of origin, but not on the same scale as it is in East Africa or the West Indies. It is unfortunate that the imported pineapple loses its flavour by the time it arrives in England. But I have a solution to that: when bought fresh from the supermarket or your local market, leave in a semi-warm place for a couple of days to settle from the stress of importation before use. Leaving it this way helps it to revive its lost flavour. The same procedure applies also to mangoes!

When you have indulged in a heavy lunch or dinner, appropriately pineapple helps the digestion process.

Ingredients:

1 small ripe pineapple
4 skewers (18cm long)
4tbsp honey
50g fresh mint, chopped

Heat grill:
Peel the pineapple and remove the middle hard core and cut into fairly big cubes (4 on each skewer). Brush with honey, place under the grill on medium heat for about 10 mins. turning occasionally. Remove from heat, garnish with mint and serve in its juices topped with ice cream.

Apart from the above recipe, pineapple has many uses, e.g. in Chinese cooking, in sandwiches/rolls or you can make a quick snack to include meat, chopped pineapples, crisp lettuce and some nuts, add a few drops of salad dressing, mix, butter the roll then pile on top of the crusty roll – "yum". There you go.

Or, if you do not fancy that, why not grill some bacon, fry mushrooms, poach an egg and grill pineapple rings for a hearty and refreshing breakfast on a Saturday or Sunday and thereafter you can relax with your favourite weekend papers. I have replaced baked beans with pineapple.

Or, buy a small tub of goats' cheese, top with chopped pineapple, chopped fresh mint, 1 tbsp honey, mix and pile on top of Ryvita or other crisp bread of your choice. This is really brilliant if you are watching your waistline.

BANANA BAKED IN GOLDEN SYRUP

Another banana recipe for you to enjoy!

Ingredients:

4 ripe firm bananas

142g double cream (whisk cream to thicken)

3tbsp golden syrup

2tbsp, rum, whisky or gin

Heat oven: 200°C/425°F/Gas mark 6

Lay the banana flat, with a sharp knife open lengthways and pry open carefully. Mix the cream, syrup and rum in a bowl. Spoon the mixture into each banana, making sure it runs through the banana without leaking. Arrange in a ceramic baking dish, cover with foil and bake for 20 mins. Remove from the oven and serve still in their skin in individual serving dishes, drizzling them with the remainder of the sauce.

BAKED BANANA IN ORANGE JUICE

Another twist to mouth-watering baked bananas.

Ingredients:

4 ripe firm bananas
4tbsp honey
Juice of one small orange
3tbp desiccated coconut
1tsp vanilla extract

Heat oven: 200°C/425°F/Gas mark 6

In a ceramic baking dish, rub some butter round dish and place the peeled bananas inside. Mix the honey with the orange juice and vanilla and pour over the bananas. Garnish with desiccated coconut and bake in a pre-heated oven for 10-15 mins.

Serve hot with ice cream.

GALIA MELON SERVED WITH MINTY ICE CREAM

Sweet Gallia melon is best served after a heavy main course, as it is so refreshing. Best served during the summer months when melons are plentiful and full of flavour.

Ingredients:

1 ripe melon – not watermelon
200g ice cream
1tsp mint sauce.

Mix the softened ice cream thoroughly with the mint sauce, put back into the fridge and leave for a couple of hours or use within 24 hours. Serve with the melon.

Cut melon in half and discard seeds. Scoop the flesh out very thinly and arrange slices on a plate overlapping each other. Top with the ice cream and serve.

CHEESE PUDDING

This is my favourite pudding and with a touch of cayenne pepper gives it that extra dimension.

Ingredients:

150g natural breadcrumbs (bought)
100g grated cheddar cheese
50g butter
½tsp black pepper
½ cayenne pepper
2 medium sized eggs, beat yolk and reserve the white
500ml full cream milk
½tsp mustard
Salt

Heat oven: 190°C/375°F/Gas mark 5

Heat up the milk, then take the pan off heat and add butter, crumbs and seasoning. Allow the ingredients to soak for about 30 mins. When ready add the egg yolk and cheese. Mix thoroughly with a wooden spoon to blend. Check seasoning. Whisk the egg white until stiff and gently fold into the mixture. Grease a ceramic pie dish and empty contents onto it. Put it straight into the oven, and bake for 30 mins..

Serve hot!

Quite yummy really.

VEGETABLES

I have devoted this section of my book to vegetables. As we all know, vegetables form an important part of our diet, especially for growing children.

Time and time again, it saddens me to hear mothers say, "My kids don't like or won't eat vegetables." Vegetables would not be poison like food to children, if only they were cooked properly. I have seen cases where vegetables are cooked until they turn a yellowish colour, especially like school dinners. No wonder, kids hate vegetables! My favourite way of cooking vegetables is by steaming, braising or roasting rather than boiling, because by doing so, the vitamins are retained. When buying vegetables see that the green ones are not yellow but a fresh green colour and crisp. Root vegetables should be firm, i.e. parsnips, carrots, etc. and if cooking, always cook quickly and drain in a colander, to avoid swimming in water.

Vegetables can be flavoured in many ways by adding different kinds of herbs of your choice, as well as butter, cheese, breadcrumbs, a little sugar, chicken stock and so on. I will show you how this can be achieved very easily with different vegetables, depending on what you are cooking.

My word of advice though regarding buying vegetables and where, for freshness, quality and quantity, has got to be your local market rather than the supermarket. You might ask, "why"? The reason being you buy cheap and fresh, value for money and enough to feed a family for a week. On the other hand, if you are a single person, supermarket is the place for you. Check what you're being sold is good quality, as market traders are in the habit of sneaking the odd bad vegetables, if you're suddenly distracted – so "beware". I get all my vegetables from the market. I believe in supporting my local vegetables market, as there are always bargains to be had.

The sky's the limit when buying seasonal vegetables, especially cabbage.

There are so many uses for cabbage that you can't go wrong if even you are a bad cook. The white variety can be used raw in salads and in coleslaw, or hot in something like a cabbage soup, which is very popular with dieters. Or you can steam it with some herbs and butter for a few minutes.

Still on the subject of vegetables, if you have room, why not create your own little herbs garden? In a disused big container in the garden, or in a window box, you can plant basil, chives, coriander, sage, parsley, etc. Seeds are easily obtainable from garden centres. Rosemary is very easy to grow and needs less attention and you can have a good crop of rosemary all year round. When using coriander in cooking, I personally tend not to discard the stems, which contain most of the flavours but reserve some of the leaves for garnishing.

Also, supermarkets now provide us with different variety of vegetables. You can also use a large disused pot in planting your own varieties. Tomatoes, carrots, Cos lettuce, rocket, courgettes, different varieties of sweet peppers.. My favourite is the red variety, which is full of sweetness. The taste of home-grown vegetables is fantastic and at least one thing you can be sure of is that they have not been sprayed with insecticides.

Finally, I hope you'll enjoy cooking and serving vegetables from your own little harvest.

Kadhu - see recipe on page 128

COOKED CARROTS

This is an easy and enjoyable way of preparing carrots that goes really well with pan-fried or grilled fish.

Ingredients:

480g carrots, peeled and cut into medium cubes
50g butter
50g coriander, chopped including the stalk
1tsp all-purpose savoury seasoning
Coarse black pepper

Boil the water in a saucepan adding a little salt. Now add the prepared carrots and cook for about 3/4 mins (be careful to keep some bite – you don't want soggy carrots!). Drain and return the carrots to the pan, adding the butter, chopped coriander and all-purpose savoury seasoning. Toss and blend well, making sure the butter has melted. Garnish with the coriander and serve immediately, while the coriander is still crisp.

MIXED VEGETABLES WITH
GREEN PESTO

The addition of the green pesto transforms the taste of the vegetables into a lovely treat that is a good accompaniment with meat dishes.

Ingredients:

3 medium carrots, peeled and cut 1cm thick
4 celery sticks, cut 1cm thick
120g button mushrooms, washed, wiped and sliced
2 tbsp olive oil or sunflower oil
1 tbsp green pesto (bought)
1 tbsp water

Heat the oil in a large saucepan over a medium heat and add all the prepared vegetables and water. Replace the lid and turn the heat down very low and cook for about 5/6 minutes without taking the lid off. Remove from heat and with the lid still on, rest for about one minute, then add the green pesto, stir well and serve straightaway.

GREEN BEANS AND
CAULIFLOWER FLORETS

This is an interesting way of preparing beans and cauliflower combined.

Ingredients:

240g dwarf green beans or French beans
1 small cauliflower (outer leaves removed), broken into small florets
50g Parmesan or Cheddar cheese (grated)
1 tbsp dried coriander or basil
50g butter
1tsp paprika pepper
2tbsp dried bacon chips (bought from supermarket)
Pinch of salt

Boil the water in a saucepan and add the beans and cauliflower. Cover then simmer gently for about 5 mins. Drain the water, replace the lid and leave to rest for about 2/3 mins so that it will cook in its own heat during that time.

Meanwhile heat the butter and add the cheese stirring until melted before finally adding the dried coriander or basil. Toss the vegetables in the butter and before serving, garnish with bacon chips and paprika.

ALTERNATIVE VERSION
CAULIFLOWER WITH PLAIN YOGHURT

Ingredients:

1 small cauliflower, broken into small florets
1tbsp natural breadcrumbs (bought in packet)
50g butter or 2tbsp olive oil
2tbsp plain yoghurt
1tsp cayenne pepper
Salt and coarse black pepper

Boil the water, add a little salt and florets and cook for about 5 mins. Drain and rest. Meanwhile melt the butter and add the breadcrumbs, yoghurt, cayenne pepper, salt and black coarse pepper. Mix well. Check seasoning. Add the florets, mix well to blend. Place under a very hot grill to brown for about 7/10 mins. Serve as a side dish.

PETIT POIS
(A pretty pea recipe)

This interesting, simple recipe is all that you need to turn kids on to the joys of vegetables! Is it any wonder they turn their noses up to the boring old boiled to within an inch of its life veggies?

Ingredients:

250g frozen peas
1 small onion, peeled and chopped
2 bacon rashers, chopped
50g butter
2tbsp flour
4 lettuce leaves, chopped
100ml water
1tbsp sesame seeds

Cover the peas and cook in the microwave on high for 5 mins. Melt butter in a saucepan and add the onion and bacon, stirring intermittently for 5 mins. Then add the flour, then water, stirring continuously to avoid any lumps. You should by now obtain a smooth consistency. Follow this by adding the cooked peas and lettuce leaves, stir for a couple of minutes and serve. Garnish with sesame seeds for extra crunchiness.

PEAS OR PETIT POIS

You can use fresh or frozen peas here.

Ingredients:

250g peas
50g butter
1tsp sugar
1tsp dried herbs of your choice
1tsp all-purpose savoury seasoning

Bring water to the boil, then add the peas with a little salt. Cook for 6 mins. Check to see they are tender enough. Drain and whilst still hot add the sugar, butter and herbs. Toss then replace the lid and leave to rest for a further 5 mins. Stir well to blend, check seasoning and serve.

COURGETTES DE LUXE

A summer vegetable that is very bland and needs a helping hand to boost the taste. Though bland, they are very versatile; they can be sliced and fried in batter, steamed to retain their crispness on the outside or tossed in herb cream or cheese. So I've come up with my very own version of cheesy courgettes. I hope you'll all enjoy it; especially your kiddiewinks that wont eat their vegetables!

Ingredients:

2 large courgettes, washed, topped and tailed and sliced lengthways, then cut 2cm thick
1tbsp Philadelphia (or other soft) cheese
1 small onion, peeled and chopped
1 clove garlic, peeled and chopped (optional)
1tbsp vegetable oil
50g chopped coriander or 2 level tsp dried herbs
1tbsp lemon juice
1 tsp paprika pepper (for a bit of bite - optional)

Heat the oil, then add the garlic and onion. Stir for a couple of minutes, then add the remainder of the ingredients, excluding the coriander. Simmer for 5 mins on a low heat - now add the coriander. Simmer for a further couple of minutes, check seasoning. And there you have it! This dish goes well as a side dish with fish or steak or as a portion of vegetables to go with whatever dish you've prepared.

ALTERNATIVE

Ingredients:

2 large courgettes, washed, topped and tailed and sliced lengthways, then cut 2cm thick
1 small onion, peeled and chopped
50g butter or 2tbsp vegetable oil
4 tomatoes, cut into wedges, deseeded and cut into little cubes
50g chopped basil or parsley
50g grated cheese
Salt and freshly ground coarse black pepper

Heat the oil, add the onion and cook for a couple of minutes. Then add the prepared courgettes. Cook on slow heat for a couple of minutes. Add the tomatoes, basil or parsley, salt and freshly ground pepper and cook for a further couple of minutes. Finish off with grated cheese, toss to blend so that the cheese melts into the courgettes. Serve whilst hot and the courgettes are still crunchy.

OR **another simple idea:**

When grated cheese has been added to the courgette, place under a hot grill to brown before serving

BROCCOLI SPEARS

This is a very quick and easy broccoli recipe of mine with the help of a microwave. Handy especially for a busy bee mummy!

Ingredients:

200g broccoli spears, wash and break into florets
1tsp all-purpose savoury seasoning
1 small red onion, cut into thin rings
50g butter
1tbsp coconut shavings (you buy this from the supermarket)
1tbsp water

In a ceramic bowl, add all the ingredients, with the exception of the coconut shavings. Cover the bowl with some cling film. Cook in the microwave on high for 6 mins. Remove, peel off cling film and stir well to blend. Now before serving, garnish with the coconut shavings.

Voila!

ALTERNATIVE – BROCCOLI SPEARS

Ingredients:

200g broccoli spears, washed and broken into florets
50g butter
1 Maggi or other chicken stock cube
1tbsp water
2tbsp crispy onion (bought from supermarket)

In a ceramic bowl, add all the ingredients, with the exception of the crispy onions, crushing the stock cube over the broccoli spears. Cover the bowl with some cling film. Cook in the microwave on high for 6 mins. Remove, peel off cling film and stir well to blend. Before serving, garnish with the crispy onions.

Enjoy!

BANANA AND CELERY SALAD

A light summer salad for your enjoyment!
Above all, I have not forgotten my vegetarian friends…

Ingredients:

1 small celery (use the inner stalks and cut into thin strips including the leaves)
½tsp white wine vinegar
1 banana, peeled and cubed
1 red sweet pepper, deseeded and cut into small cubes
½tsp crushed coarse black pepper
1 small tub of Greek yoghurt
1tsp all-purpose savoury seasoning
1tbsp crispy onions (bought from supermarket)

Mix the yoghurt and wine vinegar together. In a separate ceramic bowl, mix all the other ingredients, check seasoning, then top the salad with the yoghurt mixture, garnish with the crispy onions and serve. This goes well with grilled fish.

So refreshing!

FRIED KADHU
(*INDIAN PUMPKIN*)

Kadhu (or Kaddu) is a kind of light green Indian pumpkin or squash (see picture on page 116). It is great stir fried with herbs and served as a side dish.

Ingredients:

1 Kadhu, peeled and cubed (NB leave the seeds in)
2 cardamom pods, crushed
2tbsp vegetable oil
1 Maggi (or other) beef or chicken stock cube, crushed
1 medium onion, peeled and grated
2 garlic cloves, peeled and crushed
2 large tomatoes, skinned and deseeded
50g coriander chopped (reserve some leaves for garnishing)

Heat the oil and first add the cardamom pods, stirring for a couple of minutes. Then add the onion and garlic, followed by the Kadhu, tomatoes, coriander and crushed stock cube. With a wooden spoon, keep stirring intermittently until well blended. This should take no more than 5/10 mins. Check seasoning and serve hot.

Perfect accompaniment to well-seasoned, mouth watering rib-eye steak.

POTATO BAKE DE LUXE

A delicious potato recipe that's so uncomplicated to prepare while the dish is cooking in the oven, you can put your feet up and have a cup of tea!

Ingredients:

1kg potatoes
1 medium onion, peeled and chopped
2 garlic cloves, peeled and crushed
2 cardamom pods, crushed
200g Cheddar, grated
1 Maggi (or other) beef stock cube, dissolved in 100ml warm water
2tbsp vegetable oil

Heat oven: 200°C/400°F/Gas mark 5

Peel the potatoes, cut into ½cm slices, wash and boil for 5 mins until still firm. Meanwhile, heat the oil and fry the onion, cardamom and garlic for a couple of minutes. Now add the stock and stir. Check seasoning. Next grease an ovenproof dish with some butter, line the dish with the sliced potatoes, (overlapping) pour stock over and finally top with grated cheese. Bake in hot oven for 20/25 mins until golden brown colour.

Serve as a light supper with green seasoned salad.

MARROW STUFFED WITH ACKEE FRUIT

Marrows are not interesting vegetables. The cream-coloured flesh is very bland and because of its blandness, I have stuffed it with ackee fruit and tuna fish, and added some chilli flakes to give it that extra kick!

Ackee or Akee is a tropical West African fruit, but now grown in the West Indies as well, where it is the national fruit of Jamaica and "ackee and salt fish" is the national dish.

Ingredients:
1 medium-sized marrow
200g tinned Ackee in salted water
200g Tuna steak in brine, drain juice and reserve
100g Cheddar or Parmesan cheese, grated
½tsp chilli flakes
1 small onion, peeled and chopped finely

2 garlic cloves, peeled and chopped
2 medium sized closed chestnut mushrooms, washed and chopped
1 small sweet red or yellow pepper, deseeded and chopped
½tsp tomato puree
½tsp dried thyme or if not available, use coriander
4 streaky bacon, chopped
2tbsp vegetable or sunflower oil

Heat oven: 180°C/350°F/Gas mark 4

Top and tail marrow, peel and cut into four 3cm thick rounds, scoop out the seeds and brush some oil all over. Meanwhile, heat oil and fry bacon, onions, garlic, sweet pepper, mushrooms, chilli flakes, thyme or coriander and tomato puree and cook for about 5 minutes on medium heat, stirring intermittently. Now add the tuna and ackee, cook for a further couple of minutes. Arrange the marrow rounds on the oiled baking dish, stuff the marrow with the ackee mixture, followed by the cheese. Bake in the oven for 20/25 mins.

For the sauce: Add about 20g butter to the brine or single cream, warm through and drizzle over the stuffed marrow. Serve with green salad as a starter or as a light supper.

MARROW WRAPPED IN PANCETTA

Marrows have such watery flesh that you need some strong ingredients to give them extra flavour. So, to lighten the flavour, I have dressed it with pancetta and cheese.

Ingredients:
1 medium sized marrow
105g pancetta
100g Cheddar or Parmesan, grated
1tbsp garlic granules
Aroma all-purpose savoury seasoning and crushed black pepper

Heat oven: 200°C/400°F/Gas mark 5

Top and tail the marrow, then cut into 4cm thick slices then peel. Scoop out the seeds. Season the marrow with the savoury seasoning and black pepper. Rub some olive or vegetable oil in an ovenproof dish. Take 1 pancetta at a time and pass it through the hollowed out centre and wrap it round the marrow until covered. Garnish with cheese and place in the ovenproof dish. Bake in the oven for 20/25 mins.

Serve hot by drizzling the baked marrows with the juice from the pan, accompanied by some green salad for a light supper or as a starter.

FRIED CAULIFLOWER

This is a very straightforward way of preparing cauliflower.

Ingredients:

1 medium sized cauliflower
100g butter
4 cardamom pods, crushed
1tsp thyme
Salt and coarse black pepper

In boiling salted water, add the cauliflower whole, removing the outer green leaves and cook for 10 mins. Remove from the heat, drain, break into florets and cool. Meanwhile, heat the butter and add the cardamom and thyme and cook on medium heat to fuse flavours for a couple of minutes. Add the florets to the butter and fry, turning intermittently for about 10 mins. Season with salt and pepper. Toss. Drizzle the remaining butter from the frying pan over the cauliflower.

Serve at once with your main meal.

BAKED SWEET POTATO

Forget ordinary potatoes for now; please try my baked sweet potato.

Ingredients:

1kg white sweet potato (you cannot buy them from big supermarkets only from African or Indian supermarkets)
1tsp thyme, rosemary or cumin seeds
2tbsp vegetable oil
1tsp garlic granules
1 small onion, peeled and chopped
Salt and coarse black pepper

Heat oven: 200°C/400°F/Gas mark 5

Boil the water in a saucepan with a little salt. Meanwhile, give the potatoes a good scrub and cut into wedges (do not peel). Boil for approximately 5 mins. Drain. Mix the rest of the ingredients together and lightly toss the potatoes in the mixture, being careful not to break them. Bake in a hot oven for 30 mins.

Serve hot with whatever you fancy, instead of ordinary potatoes for a change!

STUFFED OKRA

Okra is grown widely in hot climates and is a common vegetable in Africa. Mainly used in preparing vegetable or meat broth. Eating okra is an acquired taste; you either like it or loathe it. I think the gooeyness of it can be off putting to some people. To overcome this, you need to get rid of the seeds. The seeds are the problem!

Ingredients:
250g okra (increase or reduce quantity according to taste)
100g Philadelphia (or other soft) cheese
Some melted butter
Paprika for garnishing

Heat oven: 200°C/400°F/Gas mark 5

Slit the okra lengthwise and gently scoop out the seeds. Soak in boiling water for a couple of minutes. Remove from the water and dry with kitchen paper. Stuff each okra with the cheese, brush the outer green skin with melted butter, then garnish with some paprika on each. Bake in hot oven for 15/20 mins, but no longer. Serve hot as canapés.

MISCELLANEOUS

I have devised this gravy to complement several meats including roast lamb, lamb chops, pork chops or roast pork and roast beef. These are the ingredients:

In a saucepan, add:
2tbsp Bisto (or other gravy granules)
2 cubes creamed coconut (sold in blocks). With a sharp knife cut in a sugar cube size (don't confuse with coconut cream). Readily available in supermarkets.
250ml of warm water
1tbsp white wine and cream sauce

Mix all ingredients with the stock on a medium heat, stirring all the time until everything has blended well. Check seasoning- if too thick add a little water and serve with your favourite meat.

This is my basic gravy as I prepare it and to complement it, I emptied the prepared gravy into a baking tin mixing with the sediments and meat juices. Keep stirring all the time and blend together carefully to prevent lumps. Before serving the gravy, add the following:

1. Roast lamb: 1tsp mint sauce
2. Roast beef: 1tsp tomato puree and horseradish sauce
3. Roast pork: 1tbsp applesauce

If you find the above too thick for your taste, please add some warm water, mix and serve.

My favourite way of cooking steak and with good results, is to use a heavy pan, oil it and allow it to get very hot. I sometimes make my own seasoning consisting of: (1tsp each of dried ingredients) salt, coarse black pepper, garlic salt and thyme or sage with a little oil. Mix well and rub all over the steak and allow to rest for between 15/30mins before cooking. While resting your steak, pour some water into the pan, scraping all the brown thickened juices from the bottom, adding some butter to thicken, keep stirring and pour over steak and serve.

Another way of seasoning steak that I love is to use 2 Maggi beef stock cubes, crushed, mix with some vegetable oil. Smear all over your steak and cook as above

Another accompaniment to add to steak is to serve it with butter. In a ceramic bowl mix 50g butter, ½tsp mixed herbs, ½tsp lemon juice, 1tsp coarse black pepper and form into little balls. Place in the fridge until ready to use. Place on the just cooked steak and serve immediately.

Serve grilled tomatoes with your steak for extra moistness.

The above are guides, as they allow you to prepare according to your taste.

To fry parsley for garnishing:

Wash the parsley, remove stalks and dry with kitchen paper. Meanwhile, heat some vegetable oil in a saucepan and place the parsley in a frying basket. As soon as you place the basket in the hot oil, there will be a hissing sound. Once the hissing sound stops, that means the parsley is ready. Drain and use to garnish whatever you fancy.

Introduce your children at an early age to different tastes, so that when they are a bit older it won't be a problem, especially vegetables.

Always give your children fruit juice for breakfast. Purchase fruits from the market, liquidise adding 1tbsp of lemon juice, some water and serve as part of their 5-a-day quota. Followed by cod liver oil capsules and some porridge! Drizzle honey on the porridge followed with milk and serve. Children need to line their stomachs every morning before leaving home, (no sweets or chocolates). If you fancy your porridge the Scottish way, add a little salt.

Prepare extra amount of rice, (long grain), cool, bag individually and freeze. Cooked rice freezes very well.

Time saver: prepare extra Creole sauce and freeze also – serve as usual with rice.

Wash vegetables thoroughly; do not soak in water as you lose the vitamin contents.

Wrap different cheeses separately, loosely in foil to retain freshness.

If you are serving cheese after dinner, leave the cheese out at room temperature before serving.

To put a bit of variety into your cooking, don't peel potatoes – they're much healthier served in their skins.

If you invite an Indian guest to your house for dinner, don't serve him/her with curry. Why? No matter how perfect you *think* you are, it will never taste as good as their own recipe.

If you invite *me* to your house for lunch or dinner, please don't serve me fufu and dry fish sauce, for the same reason!

Finally, my daughter Ivy does not like onions. Once I asked for her reasons and she replied, "It's like eating 'cheesy bug'". I swear I've never served her with 'cheesy bug'! I hold my hands up to say, "I'm not guilty"!